THE INDEPENDE[ ]

LONDON 2018

G. COSTA

Limit of Liability and Disclaimer of Warranty:
The publisher has used its best efforts in preparing this book, and the information provided herein is provided "as is." Independent Guides and the author make no representation or warranties with respect to the accuracy or completeness of the contents of this book and specifically disclaims any implied warranties of merchantability or fitness for any particular purpose and shall in no event be liable for any loss of profit or any other commercial damage, including but not limited to special, incidental, consequential, or other damages.

Please read all signs before entering attractions, as well as the terms and conditions of any third party companies used. Prices are approximate, and do fluctuate.

Photo Credits:
Front Cover credits: Tower Bridge (big) - UlyssesThirtyOne; Houses of Parliament - Maurice; A. Duarte, Guards – Gabriel Villena
Inside photo credits: British Museum – Rick Harris; The Royal Mews – 'Laika ac'; The Jewel Tower – David Holt; St. James's Palace – Roland Turner; Horse Guards Parade – Loco Steve; Churchill War Rooms – 'Tracey & Doug'; Heathrow – eGuide Travel; Eurostar – Loco Steve; Ferry – Roel Hemkes; People of London – Andy Roberts; Oyster Card – Amanda Slater; red London bus – Metro Centric; DLR – George Rex; Santander Cycles and London Canal Museum – Elliott Brown; Thames Clippers boat (also used on cover) – Matt Buck; Westminster Abbey – Judy Dean; Tate Britain – morebyless; The Cenotaph – Foreign and Commonwealth Office; Trafalgar Square – Christian Reimer; National Portrait Gallery – David Holt; London Transport Museum – © TfL, from London Transport Museum Collection; Somerset House – Lars Ploughmann; Royal Courts of Justice – Ronnie Macdonald; Cleopatra's Needle – Charles D P Miller; Brompton Oratory – Tony Hisgett; Saatchi Gallery and Middle Temple – Jim Linwood; Museum of London – Ewa Munro; St. Paul's Cathedral – Loco Steve; Fleet Street Dragon – Loz Pycock; Guildhall Art Gallery – Elias Gayles; Tate Modern – Chris Sampson; Shakespeare's Globe – Tom Bastin; Regent's Park – Paul Hudson; London Zoo – Kent Wang; Madame Tussauds – Karen Roe; Sherlock Holmes Museum – Anders Rasmussen; The Wallace Collection – Megan Eaves; Kew Gardens – Russell Bowes; Richmond Park – 'Jack'; Warner Bros Studio Tour and Legoland Windsor – Gary Bembridge; Hampton Court Palace – Amanda Slater; Wimbledon – Phil Whitehouse; Windsor Castle – Jean-Marc Astesana; Banqueting House – www.traveljunction.com; Westminster Cathedral – Andrew Gray; Battle of Britain London Memorial – David Holt; Imperial War Museum – Ann Lee; Ripley's – Ben Sutherland; Borough Market – Magnus D; Oxford Street – Andrew Nash; Westfield – Jim Linwood; Piccadilly and Lord's Cricket Ground – 'Dncnh'; Brick Lane – Garry Knight; Bicester Village – Neil Turner; Dominion Theatre Interior – Mario Sánchez Prada; Wembley Arena – Vinqui; Southbank Centre – Matt Brown; Wembley Stadium – Lee Thomas; Emirates Stadium – Llyod Morgan; Stamford Bridge – Jason Bagley; The Oval – Welivecricket.com; Twickenham Stadium – Marco Poggiaroni; Afternoon tea – Connie Ma; New Year's Day Parade, Pudding Race and Notting Hill Carnival – S Pahkrin; Chinese New Year – Paul; Boat Races – Robbie Shade; London Marathon – Malcolm Murdoch; Chelsea Flower Show – Karen Roe; BBC Proms – Yuichi Shiraishi; Diwali and Winter Wonderland – Garry Knight; and New Year's Fireworks – Natesh Ramasamy, Roman London - Femantlebou. Drallim (Wikicommons); Tube in 1863 - Telegraph; Blitz - New York Times; Coins - Petras Gagilas; Bank Notes - Howard Lake; Heathrow (Wide shot) - Tony Hisgett; Gatwick - Gatwick Press Office; Oyster Card Tapping In, Elizabeth Line and Bus Stop - Transport for London; Oncoming Traffic - Mike Knell; Eurotunnel - Jaguar MENA; St. Paul's and Millennium Bridge - Ed Webster; Big Ben and Westminster Bridge - DncnH; Tower Bridge on neighbourhood Guides pages - Michieru; Tower of London on neighbourhood page - Paul Pitman; London Bridge - 'mendhak'; Big Ben (cover) - Thomas Fabian; London Eye (cover) - A. Duarte; British Museum Hall (Cover) - Guillermo Viciano; Matilda - londontown.com; Victoria Sponge - Carwyn Lloyd Jones; Afternoon Tea stand - Kathryn Yengel; Stansted airport - Oleg Brovko; London City airport - James Petts; London aquarium - Neiljs; London Coliseum - VisitLondon; The Roundhouse - Wikimedia; The O2 - Dun. can; BFI - London Unveiled; Opium - Bookatable; Vista at The Trafalgar - The Telegraph; Cahoots - Time Out; Koko - GuestlistSPOT; Electric Ballroom - DIY Mag; Fabric - NME.com; The Lock Tavern - lock-tavern.com; Ye Olde Cheshire Cheese - MissLilly's Journeys; The Cross Keys - craftbeerlondon.com; Chinese New Year - Paolo Camera; West End Live - Visit London
Maps by Open Street Map (Adapted).

Contents

London: A Brief History

London is one of the most beautiful and culturally diverse places in the world with the world's fifth largest economy. The city has changed through centuries of ups and downs to become the magnificent city that it is today. This section takes a brief and interesting look at London's history.

The City Builds & Burns: Roman London (43 to 410 AD)

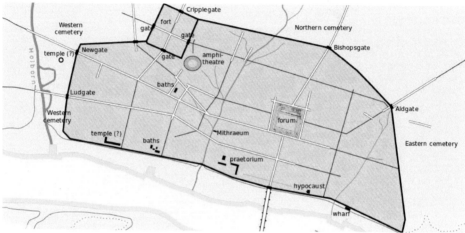

Today's London started off as a civilian town called Londinium, established by the Romans a few years after the invasion of AD43.

Londinium is believed to have been equivalent to the size of Hyde Park today, and the Roman army built a sturdy wooden bridge over the Thames, east of where today's London Bridge is situated. As a result of the bridge and construction of roads from the Londinium port, there was an influx of merchants, traders and other urban dwellers in search of better living conditions and opportunities.

Over the next few years,

Londinium prospered and became an important town but this came to a halt when in 60AD, Queen Boudicca, of the Icene tribe of Norfolk, targeted Londinium as a show of her antagonism of Roman rule. Boudicca and her army razed Londinium to the ground, killing thousands in the process, and as a result orchestrated one of the first recorded burnings of London in history. The buildings at the time were made of wood and clay and therefore burnt very easily.

After the invasion of Boudicca, it did not take long for the Romans to re-establish control. The strategic location of

Londinium made it too valuable to forfeit, therefore it was hastily rebuilt. It became a walled and planned Roman city. The rebirth was the beginning of a golden era of trade and by 100AD, large amounts of goods were being traded in Londinium – emanating from, and going to, extensive corners of the empire.

Luxury goods such as pottery, wine, olive oil, marble and slaves became rampant in Londinium through import from Spain, Italy, Gaul and Greece, while a viable export market for tin, silver, copper, oysters, corn and woollen cloak was established.

London's Fortune Changes: Roman London Ends

Londinium boasted an amphitheatre, a temple, a palace, bath houses and a large fort at its peak but as the proverb says "every beginning must have an end".

During the visit of Emperor Hadrian in 122AD, it was estimated that Londinium had a population of about 45,000 and was largely perceived as a cultural melting point, due to its cosmopolitan mix. However, by the 3rd century, Londinium's fortunes began to change as a result of several factors, including: political instability in the empire, recession, and barbarian and pirate attacks.

Over the next century, soldiers were constantly pegged away from Britannia to deal with barbarian attacks elsewhere and Emperor Constantine II recalled the last troops in 407 AD. A few years later, Emperor Honorius declined requests from Britain for military aid and this officially marked the end of Roman rule, thereby setting in motion the end of Roman London. By the middle of the 5th century, Londinium was completely deserted and abandoned.

The Viking Invasion

When the Romans left, London ceased to be an important town and it fell into obscurity. However, London's location on the Thames was important, so the 7th century witnessed trade expand and the city flourished once more.

The growth was stable and free flowing, and as a result, by the 9th century, London became a prosperous trading center and its affluence attracted the attention of the Danish Vikings, who in 851 attacked and destroyed the city.

It is believed that the English, Danish and then Norman kings had control of the city during the 10th century.

By 1014, while the Danish controlled the city, a large force of Norwegian Vikings and Anglo-Saxons attacked London, leading to the fall of London Bridge – still a popular, and well-known, nursery rhyme today.

When Danish King Cnut ascended to power in 1017, attacks ceased due to Cnut's willingness to unite Anglo-

Saxons with the Danes and the invitation of Danish merchants to settle in the city.

Until King Cnut's death, London prospered but his demise reverted the city back to Anglo-Saxon rule under Edward the Confessor.

London became the largest city in England and the most prosperous in Britain, but it was not the capital: Winchester held that role until the 12th century.

Disaster: The Plague and the Great Fire

By the 1600s, the growth and continued expansion of London led an influx of all classes and many people lived in extreme poverty.

As people disposed of their waste (both organic and human) out in the streets of the city, London became filthy and infested with rats and fleas.

In 1665, the early victims of The Great Plague were first discovered in the poorer areas of London due to the deplorable living conditions. The spread of the plague was aided by overpopulation, which encouraged close contact between healthy and infected people, and even contact with rats and fleas. The disease spread quickly;

the rich relocated to the countryside for safety while the poor stayed put.

As a response to the disease, new laws were created to help curb the spread of the plague: the military guarded certain areas, red crosses were painted on the doors of the infected, dogs were killed, and searchers hunted down dead bodies for mass burials. The winter halted the spread of the plague as the cold took its toll on the rats and fleas.

Though the real tragedy had passed by the tail end of 1665, the demise of the disease was in part due to the Great Fire of London in 1666.

The fire - started in a bakery on Pudding Lane - destroyed the infested areas where rats had multiplied. The fire was reported to have burnt down over 13,000 houses, 88 parish churches, and left over 70,000 inhabitants of London homeless.

Only 6 people were reported to have been killed in the fire which lasted from the 2nd to 5th September 1666.

The rebuilding of the city after The Great Fire was swift; King Charles appointed commissioners including Christopher Wren

to supervise the rebuild.

These supervisors determined the length of streets, quality of materials and positioning of important public structures such as markets, churches, and secular buildings.

Wren's grand plan for London was never used, but by the end of 1670, over 6000 houses had been built.

Christopher Wren, who was knighted in 1673, supervised the construction of fifty-one parish churches, including the masterpiece that is St Paul's Cathedral.

Another notable name in the rebuilding of London is John Nash, who designed Buckingham Palace, Marble Arch and Regent Street.

The Bank of England was established towards the end of the 17th century, and by now London handled 80% of England's imports and almost 70% of its exports.

It should be noted that London was not a place where goods were manufactured, but mainly a place where goods were traded.

Politics, The Industrial Revolution & The Railways

In 1707, the Kingdom of Great Britain came to be as the English and Scottish parliaments came together with the Acts of Union. London at the time was expanding rapidly: in the west towards Mayfair, the east saw an expansion of the Port of London, and bridges across the river allowed London to grow towards the south.

A new phenomenon in London at the time was the coffeehouse where people gathered to read newspapers as printing

presses became common. Fleet Street became synonymous with news.

Eighteenth century London was also rife with crime with the death penalty being using for the vast majority of wrongdoings. Public hangings, in areas such as Marble Arch, were common and big public spectacles.

London went through a radical change in the 1800s. It became the world's largest city and during the 19th century its population exploded from 1 million to

6.7 million.

During the 19th century, the invention of the steam train and its railways, under Queen Victoria's reign transformed London, but the construction of new railways meant the demolition of many buildings, mostly in poor areas due to the easy approval by government authorities.

London's maiden railway line was commissioned in February 1836 between Deptford and Bermondsey.

The 1840s, experienced railway boom, with the arrival of long distance railway travel. The introduction of the railways saw a massive rise in population and London's area continued to expand.

A few years later, in 1863, London unveiled the world's first underground railway running from Paddington to Farringdon.

Meanwhile, in 1855, Joseph Bazalgette led a team of workers who constructed over 2,000km of tunnels in London's first sewage system. The death rate in London dropped dramatically as living

conditions improved.

London's population began to become more international, as Irish settlers arrived during the Great Famine in the mid-

1850s. People from poorer parts of Europe emigrated to London, as did many from colonial countries.

World Wars and 20th Century London

London suffered heavily during World War I but was still the capital of a massive empire. Between the two World Wars, London expanded geographically as the transport system grew and allowed people to live in the suburbs; car ownership also facilitated this.

Unemployment grew rapidly during the Great Depression of the 1930s, only to be followed by World War II. During The Blitz, London suffered extensive damage, and again fires raged through the City of London destroying it. Over one million houses in London were destroyed, and the death toll reached 40,000. Many escaped to the countryside, fearing for their lives.

London went through an enormous rebuilding

project after WWII, and the 1950s and 1960s saw big tower blocks being built to house Londoners. During this time, many immigrants came to the city from the Commonwealth countries – Indians, Jamaicans, Pakistanis and Bangladeshis made their way to the city, making it a truly multicultural place.

London's population was decreasing, though, and had dropped from 8.6 million

before WWII to 6.8 million in the 1980s. This began to increase again from the mid-1980s onwards.

Today, London's population stands at 8.8 million. The city boasts four world heritage sites, the world's premier financial district, the top spot for international tourism, countless high-quality educational institutions and residents from all around the globe.

Know Before You Go

London is a fascinating city: it is a place where people from all walks of life and cultures live together; it is a global economic powerhouse with the City of London's Stock Exchange and Canary Wharf; and it is a historic city that still thrives to this day.

The People of London: Demographics

London's cultural background is very diverse.

45% of people in London are of a White British origin, 15% are other White, 18% are Asian, 13% are Black, 5% are Mixed and 4% classify themselves as 'Other'.

In terms of wealth, London is a city of two extremes. Travelling through central London's areas such as Mayfair and Kensington, it is not uncommon to walk past homes worth £30 million or more.

Outside the wealthy areas, you will discover that 27% of Londoners are officially classified as living in poverty.

This is a city with people of all ages, backgrounds and wealth.

Local Customs and Etiquette

Tipping

Tipping practices vary wildly across the world, and in London there are certain rules to abide by. You should follow the UK tipping practices and not those of your home country.

Every person In employment in the UK earns at least the minimum wage. As of late 2017, this is £7.05 an hour for those aged 21 and over, and £7.50 for those aged at least 25. For those aged 18 to 20, it is £5.60 an hour. This is on par with many other major nations. Every employer is required to pay their employees at least the minimum wage, and tips cannot be used to make up the minimum wage.

However, in order to have a "normal standard of living", there is also a "living wage". This is a non-compulsory advisory for employers who wish to ensure their

employees can afford to live in the city. Employers may choose the pay this on a voluntary basis. The London Living Wage is currently £10.20 an hour.

Most people you will come into contact with in customer-focused roles do not earn the £10.20 living wage and likely earn the minimum wage – the gap between the two pay levels is at least £2.50 per hour, for 18 to 20 year olds the

minimum wage is just over half of the living wage. Therefore, many people rely on tips in order to make up the rest of their income.

The cost of living in London is extremely high, and therefore tips make a major difference to many people - more than in the rest of the UK.

Tips are NOT compulsory in the UK on any service. If a service charge is added to a bill without it being stated beforehand (such as on a menu), you can legally request that it be removed. However, as most employees in customer-service roles have very low wages, tips are very much appreciated.

In the UK the most common tip is at a restaurant. Here a 12.5% to 15% tip on the final price of the bill is the norm. If a restaurant has added on a "service charge", that is the tip.

It is bad form to not tip if you received a good level of service, but tips are – of course – optional. In London, people do not tip at fast food locations or for take-away meals. You may choose to tip £1 or £2 for a food delivery. Tips in bars and pubs are also not commonplace.

Taxi services merit the second most common form of tip. Here 10% is more than enough; most people will round up to the nearest £1 or £5 to avoid the taxi driver searching for change.

In the hospitality industry, it is becoming increasingly common to tip for help from a hotel's concierge or for help with luggage. Here a small tip is highly appreciated – £1 to £3 is more than enough. This is still not the norm for everyone at the moment.

Finally, if you are on an

excursion, walking tour, bus tour or private guided tour, tips are commonplace for these. A tip of £3 to £5 is a nice gesture for an enjoyable tour. Day-long group tours may warrant a tip of £5 or £10, and if you have had a private, custom tour 10% to 20% of the tour price is common.

Public transport
On the public transport system, the "metro", "subway" or "underground", is the tube - pronounced 'chewb' (not 'toob').

The tube also has its own etiquette. For example, do allow people off the train before boarding. On escalators inside stations, you stand on the right and allow people to walk on the left.

Once on a train, if you are seated, you should give up your seat to any disabled, elderly or pregnant passengers.

Trains are only at stations for a few seconds and it is, therefore, customary to be ready to leave the train before it stops at a station.

Tube etiquette dictates that you avoid eye contact with the person sat opposite you or anyone else on the carriage. Transport for London, has devised the clever placing of advertisements just above the seats for this very purpose. Better still, close

your eyes and plug in your earphones, or bring a book.

Shopping
When asking for something, the phrase is "May I have.." or "Could I have" but never "I need..." or "I want...".

Accents
Many people in London have an accent known as received pronunciation (RP), also known as the Queen's English or BBC English. However, as Londoners are people from all backgrounds, you will likely encounter a wide variety of accents throughout your stay.

Americanisms
Americanisms (American versions of British words) are not used in London. If you're asking for the restroom, a corndog, an elevator, the subway, where the start of the 'line' is, asking for 'the check', or other non-British words, this can cause confusion.

In the hospitality trade, most employees are aware and used to hearing American English. In other places, you may well be asked what these words mean.

Learning a few British English words and phrases can make a big difference to your visit to London. On the next page is our guide to some of the common British phrases you may hear or use.

Useful Phrases

British English	International English
Tube (said 'chewb')	Metro, Subway or Underground
Subway	Underground walkway beneath a road
Toilet	Bathroom or Restroom
Chips	Fries (thick cut, like 'steak fries' in the US)
Crisps	Chips (like Lays, McCoys, Walkers)
Ground Floor	First Floor
"Taking the piss" (colloquial)	To mock someone or something
Ground Floor	First Floor
First Floor	Second Floor (etc.)
Biscuit	Cookie
Sweets	Candy
Note	Bill
Bill	Check
Queue	Line
Jumper/Hoodie	Sweater
Mobile Phone	Cell Phone
Trainers	Sneakers

Making Calls

Make sure your mobile phone will work in the UK before visiting. Modern smartphones will most likely work everywhere. However, some older models, and non-smartphones, may be limited to your home country or region. Be sure to check before travelling. Your phone network or carrier may also require you to have an international roaming plan set up in advance.

Beware of roaming charges when visiting the UK. Calls and text messages will often cost significantly more than they do back home. You may also be charged to receive calls and messages too. Data, in particular, can be extremely expensive so check with your network provider whether they offer any roaming deals or packages.

Once in the UK, to dial another UK number (to make a restaurant reservation for example) you do not need to worry about dialling codes and merely need to call the number you see on publicity. Phone numbers in the UK generally begin with 01 if outside London, and 02 within London.

If you need to make international phone calls, you may need to enter your country's international dialling code, followed by the phone number. For the USA, for example, you would need to add +1 (or 001) before the phone number.

Currency

In the UK, the Pound Sterling is used as the form of currency. Although, the UK is currently part of the European Union, where many countries use the Euro (€), the UK has not adopted this currency.

One pound is written as £1. This is sub-divided into 100 pennies, 'p' or pence – these terms are used interchangeably. Coins available in the UK are 1p, 2p, 5p, 10p, 20p, 50p, £1 and £2.

Paper currency are called 'notes'. These are available in denominations of £5, £10, £20 and £50. £50 notes are sometimes not accepted at smaller stores due to their high value and fear of forgery, so try to avoid them when exchanging your cash. Sometimes a manager may be called to verify £50 notes before they are accepted, even at larger stores. All coins and notes bare the head of Queen Elizabeth II.

Fun Tip: New coin designs are issued regularly, so be sure to check the back of your coins. The most elaborate designs are on £2 coins; you may come across a design of St. Paul's Cathedral, the Magna Carta, or even a commemoration of World War I, amongst dozens of others.

Weather

London experiences the four seasons, so the timing of your visit has a large impact what clothes to pack, as well as the activities you may wish to do.

The coldest month is usually February with an average low of 2 °C (35 °F), but with occasional drops below freezing in both January and February. Snowfall varies: some years there is none; other years, London's transport system comes to a halt with a few inches it.

Summer has average highs lying around 22 °C (72 °F), though the city environment makes it feel much warmer. Even at these temperatures the non-air conditioned underground lines are swelteringly hot. Some days in the summer may see temperatures top 30 °C (85 °F), and summer 2015 saw highs of 36 °C (97°F). In the evenings, temperatures cool down quickly, so carry a light jumper or hoodie.

Spring and Autumn are similar. From March to June, and September to November, expect highs of between 10°C and 20°C, and lows between 4°C and 11°C.

Rainfall is relatively consistent throughout the year, with monthly rainfall averaging between 46mm (1.7") and 77mm (3"). Each month has 9 to 12 rainy days on average, and Autumn is the wettest season. February is the month with the least rain, but only marginally; averages say that October is the wettest month.

Month by Month Temperature Averages:

Temperatures are averages, in Celsius, followed by Fahrenheit.

Month	Low (C/F)	High (C/F)	Month	Low (C/F)	High (C/F)
January	2/35	7/44	July	13/55	22/72
February	2/35	7/44	August	13/55	22/72
March	4/39	11/52	September	11/51	19/66
April	5/41	13/55	October	8/46	15/59
May	8/46	17/63	November	5/41	10/50
June	11/51	20/68	December	3/37	7/44

Internet Access

London has excellent mobile phone signal for data and calls across all networks. However, data access can be very expensive for international visitors, so you are best sticking to Wi-Fi hotspots.

Most hotels include unlimited Wi-Fi in the cost of your room. McDonald's, Pret a Manger and Starbucks provide free Wi-Fi access at their locations, as do Apple Stores. Most coffee shops and restaurants also provide free Wi-Fi, although you may have to ask for an access code or register your details.

The City of London area is covered with free street-wide Wi-Fi almost everywhere too.

Virgin Media provides free Wi-Fi on the tube at stations and platforms for some UK mobile phone users; there are also paid access passes available. Many public libraries and museums also provide free access.

Important: You will need plug adapters that work in the UK. These are NOT the same as in the rest of Europe. The UK uses a three-pronged design, as opposed to continental Europe's two prongs.

Also, be sure to check the voltage of your devices before bringing them. The UK runs on 230-240V unlike some regions' 100V (e.g. the US), so you will need a power inverter for some items. If you plug the 100V items in directly with an adapter but not an inverter, they will likely burn or blow.

Many items are now able to be connected without an inverter, and simply require an adapter. Check the power brick of your appliance and make sure it supports either 230V or 240V. Continental European items usually run on 230V, so an adapter is required for these due to the plug shape, but not a power inverter.

Clothing Sizes

Clothing sizes in the UK differ both from those in the US and in Continental Europe.

These tables cover everything from shoe size to shirt size. Note that sizes may differ between men and women as stated.

Women's dresses

UK	US	Europe
2	0	28
4	2	30
6	4	32
8	6	34
10	8	36
12	10	38
14	12	40
16	14	42

Women's shoes

UK	US	Europe
3	4.5	36
4	5.5	37
5	6.5	38
6	7.5	39
7	8.5	40
8	9.5	41

Men's trousers

UK and US	Europe
30	46
32	48
34	50
36	52
38	54
40	56
42	58

Men's suits and jackets

UK and US	Europe
34	44
36	46
38	48
40	50
42	52
44	54
46	56

Men's shirts (collar)

UK and US	Europe
14	35
14.5	36-37
15	38
15.5	39-40
16	41
16.5	42-43
17	44

Men's shoes

UK	US	Europe
8	8.5	42
8.5	9	42.5
9	9.5	43
9.5	10	43.5
10	10.5	44
10.5	11	44.5

Getting to London

Before you begin to explore the city, you must first get here. This section covers your options on reaching England's capital.

Flying

As the UK is a fairly isolated island, most visitors who arrive in London, do so by plane. The airports in London, when combined, make up the largest city airport system in the world, carrying the highest number of passengers. When flying into London, there are five main airports to consider. These are listed in size below, with the largest first.

LONDON HEATHROW AIRPORT

Heathrow is the busiest airport in Europe in terms of passenger traffic and the most popular in London. It is located 22km from central London, or 12 miles. It has five terminals, of which four are operational. Terminal 1 is closed. The airport has two runways.

Public Transport
Underground – The Piccadilly line on the London Underground goes between Heathrow and central London with stops at all airport terminals. Journey times are about 40 to 60 minutes between central London and the airport.

The cash fare between central London and Heathrow is £6. The Oyster Card or Contactless payment fare is £3.10 off-peak, and £5.10 during peak hours. This is the most affordable rail option (more on public transport tickets in the next chapter).

Heathrow Express – A non-stop National Rail train taking 15 minutes from Heathrow Central (Terminals 2 and 3) to London Paddington Station. Trains depart every 15 minutes. The journey time to Terminal 5 is 21 minutes.

There is a free shuttle train between Heathrow Central and Terminal 4 – the journey lasts just 4 minutes.

A same-day adult fare is £25 one-way or £37 return for standard class. Children 15 and under travel free with a fare-paying adult. Tickets booked in advance can be as low as £5.50 one-way and £11 return. If you are staying in the Paddington area, want a speedy transfer, and can book in advance, the Express service offers great value for money. From May 2018, you are able to use Oyster Cards on this service, paying £25.

Heathrow Connect (until May 2018) – A National Rail service taking 27 minutes from Heathrow Central to London Paddington station. It follows the same route as the Heathrow Express, but with up to five stops along the way. Trains run every 30 minutes and serve Heathrow Terminals 2 and 3. For Terminal 4, a free shuttle train is available.

Passengers travelling to Terminal 5 need to take free bus transportation from inside the terminal (not the rail station). If you are travelling to Terminal 5, we do not recommend this.

One-way tickets between Heathrow and Paddington are £10.30, or £20.70

return. Heathrow Connect will cease operation in May 2018 - an exact end date is not yet available.

TfL Rail (from May 2018)
- This replaces Heathrow Connect from May 2018. It will offer 4 trains per hour and a journey time of 23 minutes between Heathrow Central and Paddington. Fares are expected to the be same as the London Underground (£3.10 off-peak, and £5.10 during peak hours) with Oyster Cards and Contactless payments or £6 in cash. An exact start date is not yet available.

Elizabeth Line (from May 2019) - This new rail line will run from all Heathrow terminals to Paddington and many other locations throughout London. Oyster Cards and Contactless payments will be accepted, with prices the same as the London Underground. Trains run every 10 to 20 minutes.

Bus/Coach – All services arrive and depart from Heathrow Central Bus station (Terminals 2 and 3). Some also operate from bus stations at Terminals 4 & 5.

National Express and Oxford Bus Company both operate services between Heathrow and London Victoria Coach station. Green Line route 724 goes to St. Alban's.

The journey time is 45 to 60 minutes in normal conditions, and up to 2 hours in traffic. Coaches are £6 to £8 booked in advance.

If travelling between midnight and 5:00am, night-bus route N9 operates, taking you to various

locations in central London including Hammersmith and Trafalgar Square. The price is £1.50 on an Oyster or by Contactless payment. Buses do not take cash.

Other Transport

Car – Driving into central London is not recommended. Public transport is excellent, and running a car is expensive.

If you insist on driving, follow directions to the Heathrow area exit tunnel and then follow the M4 motorway to central London. Make sure you have a map or GPS device as London is a large and complicated city.

The journey takes 45 to 60 minutes to central London if you do not encounter traffic. This journey time can double in rush hour traffic.

Taxi – A ride in a black taxi (cab) to central London will typically take 30 to 60 minutes depending on location, with no traffic. The fare is typically £45 to £85.

There are no extra charges for luggage or additional passengers. A £2.80 charge applies for taxi journeys starting at Heathrow.

All taxis will take card payments, as well as cash.

Minicabs – These must be booked in advance; it is illegal to take a minicab that has not been pre-booked. Drivers will usually meet you at the flight arrivals area in the terminal. Heathrow Airport officially recommends greentomatocars.com who use hybrid cars. Book online or call +44(0)208 568 0022 for a quote.

Uber – This is a popular option, allowing you to book a car from your smartphone on demand. There are several categories of car to choose from. You will get an estimated price before you confirm your vehicle – estimates range from £29 to £94 one-way. Get $20/£10 free credit by using our exclusive sign-up link at uber.com/invite/uberindependentguides or enter "uber independentguides" (without spaces) as a voucher code when using the app for the first time.

Taxis, Uber and Minicabs can be especially good value for groups.

LONDON GATWICK AIRPORT

Gatwick is London's second largest airport and is located 29.5miles (47.5km) from central London, about twice as far out as Heathrow. It has two terminals (North and South) and one runway. It is the world's busiest "single-use runway" airport. Both terminals are connected by a shuttle train.

Public Transport

Gatwick Express – A non-stop train taking 30 minutes between Victoria Station in central London and the airport; trains run every 15 minutes. Standard Class tickets are £19.90 each way for adults, £35.50 return, or £9.95 each way for children, £17.75 return. First Class tickets are £29.70 for adults and £14.85 for children each way, or £57.50 and £28.75 respectively return.

A discount of 10% is available online. You can also use contactless payment and Oyster Cards instead of a physical ticket. Fares are the same price as the on-the-day fare.

Other Train Services – Southern Railways and Thameslink provide services between Gatwick Airport and central London. Trains make more stops than the Gatwick Express but are much cheaper. There are a wider variety of starting points for your journey: London Victoria, London Bridge, London Charing Cross, London Waterloo East, City Thameslink, London Blackfriars, London Kings Cross and London Liverpool Street. Journey times range from 30 to 53 minutes.

Single adult fares vary based on which departure time and station. These range between £9.50 and £15.50 for a one-way single ticket in standard class for adults. Single child fares vary between £4.75 and £10.

We recommend this over the Gatwick Express as the savings can be substantial, especially for a group. Purchase "Anytime" tickets online or at the station. "Advance" tickets only allow you to travel on a certain train which could be missed due to flight, immigration or baggage delays.

Coach/Bus – National Express coaches from Victoria Coach Station to Gatwick Airport cost about £8 each way, with a journey time of 1 hour 5 minutes to 1 hour 25 minutes.

EasyBus tickets start at £2 each way if booked far in advance from Earl's Court to Gatwick with a journey time of about 1 hour 5 minutes.

Terravision is another operator with fares from £6.

Other Transport

Car – Follow the M23 and A23 towards London for about 23 miles to the edge of central London. Follow B221 towards Westminster and local signs from there. The drive to Westminster is about 1 hour 30 minutes. The drive is long and expensive; a train is usually a better option.

Taxi – Gatwick's official service is "Airport Cars Gatwick" which can be booked online at taxis.gatwickairport.com/bookings/taxi.html.

A pre-booked minicab usually costs £45 to £60 each way. A local black taxi costs over £100 each way.

Uber – Another popular option, allowing you to book a cab from your smartphone on demand. There are several categories of car. You will get an estimated price before you book.

Fares generally run between £79 and £130 one-way depending on location. Get $20/£10 free credit by using our exclusive sign-up link at uber.com/invite/uberindependentguides or enter "uber independentguides" (without spaces) as a voucher code when using the app for the first time.

LONDON STANSTED AIRPORT

Stansted Airport lies 30 miles, or 48 kilometres, north-east of central London. It is the newest large passenger airport in London.

Stansted is a breeze to get through with a beautiful glass terminal with lots of natural light, making it feel spacious. It is not as busy as Gatwick and Heathrow airports.

This airport is mainly targeted at European travellers, though a few flights to long-haul destinations have been added in recent years. It is, however, still a major airport with over 19 million passengers a year traveling through it.

Public Transport

Stansted Express Train – Departs every 15 minutes with a journey time of 47 minutes between London Liverpool Street and the airport. You can also get the Stansted Express from Stratford (with a change at Tottenham Hale) or directly from Tottenham Hale station in east London.

Same-day tickets are £18 to £19 each way (depending on your start point), or £30 to £32 return for adults. First class fares are £10 more expensive each way and include a FastTrack airport security pass.

Pre-booked tickets start at £7.50 each way – you must specify a travel date, but not a time. Group offers are also available for parties of 3 or 4 passengers.

Coach – National Express coach tickets start at £6 per person each way with journey times of 1 hour 30 minutes to 1 hour 45 minutes. EasyBus tickets start at £2 per person each way with journey times of approximately 1 hour 15 minutes to 1 hour 30 minutes. Terravision also runs serves between the airport and Stratford, Victoria Coach Station, Baker Street and Liverpool Street.

Other Transport

Car – Join the M11 at Junction 8, follow the M11 until you reach the North Circular road (A406). You are now in East London. Please have a navigation device with you for the rest of the journey as it very much depends on where you would like to go in London itself.

We do not recommend driving for most people as it is a long drive (over an hour) and can be done far more quickly by train.

Taxi and Uber – We do not recommend you take a taxi to and from your hotel due to the long journey time and expense. A train will usually be a much better option. In a cab, the journey will take 70 to 80 minutes and will cost about £95 to £110. There is no taxi rank at the airport; these must be pre-booked in advance with London Black Cabs. This can be done at arrivals. A mini cab may be cheaper.

An Uber between the airport and central London is priced at between £58 and £119 depending on the size of car you request, and where you are travelling to.

Get $20/£10 free credit by using our exclusive sign-up link at uber.com/invite/uberindependentguides or enter "uber independentguides" (without spaces) as a voucher code when using the app for the first time.

LONDON LUTON AIRPORT

London Luton is another of London's airports and it consists mainly of low-cost carriers from across Europe. There are some charter routes out of the airport to North Africa, New York and Asia but these are few and far between. Luton is 35 miles or 56.5km north of central London.

One of the big advantages with Luton is its size – because it is still relatively small, you can get through the airport quite quickly. It still, however, sees over 10.5 million passengers come through its doors every year and is growing rapidly.

Public Transport

Rail – Journeys from central London to "Luton Airport Parkway" station are operated by Thameslink and East Midland Trains. Trains are available from London Blackfriars and London St. Pancras stations. Journey times vary considerably – there is one fast train per hour from St. Pancras where the journey time is a mere 20 minutes. Other journeys vary from 39 to 55 minutes.

Luton has an unusual situation where the rail station is not directly located in the airport itself; instead it is 1 mile west of the airport, and both are linked by a shuttle bus that runs every 10 minutes during the day. The shuttle bus journey takes an additional 10 minutes and costs £2.10 each way or

£3.40 return if your train tickets are booked to "Luton Airport Parkway". Train tickets booked to "Luton Airport" include the shuttle bus fare.

Coach – Terravision, National Express and EasyBus all provide shuttle services from central London directly to London Luton airport. Transfer time is 50 to 80 minutes depending on where you board. Prices are generally between £8 and £12 each way. Promotional fares from £2 are sometimes available, if booked well in advance.

Other Transport

Car – This is a fairly easy car journey with a typical journey time of 45 minutes to 1 hour 15 minutes depending on traffic. From Luton Airport, you will need to follow signs for the M1 motorway going south, when in the suburbs of London, you will briefly join

the A406 (North Circular Road). Then exit onto the A41 (Hendon Way), and finally follow Finchley Road to reach central London. From here, we recommend you use a GPS device to reach your destination.

Taxi and Uber – You can get a black London cab directly from the taxi rank outside the main terminal. You can also make a reservation with one of the many mini-cabs firms that operate.

With an Uber, expect to pay between £50 and £129 for the journey depending on what type of car you get and the destination.

Get $20/£10 free credit by using our exclusive sign-up link at uber.com/invite/uberindependentguides or enter "uber independentguides" (without spaces) as a voucher code when using the app for the first time.

LONDON CITY AIRPORT

This is the most centrally located of all the airports, being only 6 miles from central London, making it a breeze to get to. It is small and caters mostly for business travellers.

Its destinations are mostly short haul in Europe, as well as New York. This airport also has great connections across the UK.

Just 3.6 million passengers use the airport yearly, and it is the least busy of London's airports.

Due to the short runway length and its location, the airplanes used here are all relatively small – the largest takes just 132 passengers.

Public Transport

DLR – Transport for London operates the DLR, which is integrated with the Underground system. Bank Station to London City Airport is only 22 minutes on the DLR with fantastic views of East London along the way. Oyster Card and contactless card fares are £3.30 during peak times, and £2.80 off-peak. The cash fare is £4.90.

Other Transport

Driving – We do not recommend driving to London City Airport and around London in general. Avis, Budget, Europcar and Hertz operate rental locations at the airport. The driving time will take between 35 minutes and 1 hour depending on where you are going in central London.

Taxi and Uber – Taxi prices are metered from London City Airport to central London. Expect to pay about £35 each way between the airport and Covent Garden, £40 to Piccadilly and £50 to Bayswater. Uber prices average £20 to £30 from most places in central London.

If you are using Uber, get $20/£10 free credit by using our exclusive sign-up link at uber.com/invite/uberindependentguides or enter "uber independentguides" (without spaces) as a voucher code when using the app for the first time.

Ferries and Cruises

Ferry and cruises services are available into ports around the UK, with several locations a short drive from London. Ferries carry your vehicle, as well as passengers, between the UK and the rest of Europe.

Many coach companies also use the Ferry services to access the UK on excursions between London and Continental Europe. Many cruises around Europe also commence and end in ports near London.

Calais (France) to Dover (England) is the shortest ferry trip at just 90 minutes. Dunkirk (France) to Dover is another option – this trip is about 2 hours on the ferry.

Ferries between France and Spain, arriving into the UK ports of Portsmouth, Poole and Plymouth are also available. These are longer ferry journeys ranging from 6 hours to an overnight trip with a sleeping cabin onboard.

Finally, ferry crossings from Rotterdam (The Netherlands) and Esbjerg (Denmark) are also available. Rotterdam is a 6-hour crossing, and Esbjerg is an 18-hour crossing.

Expect to pay at least £100 for a car transfer from Portsmouth to central London (1h45-2h drive), and £250-£300 from Plymouth to central London (4h drive). Cheaper non-private shuttles may be available.

Rail to London

NATIONAL RAIL

If you are travelling across the UK to London, you will arrive in one of the main terminals. These are:
• **Paddington** (to and from Oxford, Bristol, South Wales, Bath, Exeter, Plymouth)
• **Marylebone** (Warwick and all Euston's destinations)
• **Euston** (Birmingham, North Wales, Liverpool, Manchester, Glasgow and Scotland)
• **St. Pancras** (Leicester, Nottingham, Sheffield, Leeds and Dover)
• **Kings Cross** (Leeds, York, Newcastle, Edinburgh and Scotland)
• **Liverpool Street** (Norwich and Cambridge)
• **Charing Cross** (Dover)
• **Waterloo** (Brighton, Portsmouth, Southampton, Exeter)
• **Victoria** (Brighton and Dover)

All these stations are in Zone 1 in central London. You will likely need the tube or a taxi to get to your final destination.

EUROTUNNEL

London is connected to continental Europe via a 50km rail link (the Channel Tunnel or 'Chunnel') that connects Folkestone in south-east England with Calais in the north of France. The journey time is about 35 minutes.

You can drive a lorry, car, motorhome or motorbike onto the Eurotunnel train which then travels through the Channel Tunnel. The crossing time is just 35 minutes and it is a fantastic and fast way to get between the continent and the UK.

Prices vary on the length of trip: a one-day or overnight trip begins at £23 each way; a 5-day trip starts at £59; other trips start at £76 each way. This can work out to be a very affordable price per passenger. Prices are per vehicle and include all passengers inside it.

The Eurotunnel terminal at Folkestone is a 75-mile drive from central London (1 h 45 m to 2h driving time).

EUROSTAR

The Eurostar is a high-speed passenger train between London and mainland Europe.

You check-in for your Eurostar train at least 30 minutes before departure. This is simply a case of scanning your ticket at the automated barriers.

Then you will go through airport-style security (you *can* bring liquids with you) with a metal detector and an X-Ray baggage scan. This is followed by passport control a. You will board your train when it is announced in the lounge.

On Eurostar services, you take all luggage with you and must be able to physically carry this onto the train. When you reach the other end, you simply step off the train.

Travel times and prices:
• London to Calais – 1 hour 5 minutes, £58
• London to Lille – 1 hour 20 minutes, £58
• London to Brussels – 1 hour 51 minutes, £58
• London to Paris – 2 hours 15 minutes, £58
• London to Disneyland Paris – 2 hour 35 minutes, £76

Journey times stated above are for the fastest trains. Slower trains may take a few extra minutes. The prices are 'starting at' return prices for one adult. Child and youth fares will save you a few pounds each way.

Prices increase as seats sell out. Occasional sales are also available during slower periods of the year.

There are also 'direct' services from London to the south of France – destinations include Lyon, Avignon and Marseille, as well as a seasonal ski service. Eurostar will also begin a direct service between London and Amsterdam in Spring 2018.

Transport in London

Transport has always been, and will always be, fundamental to London. The city is large and getting 8.6 million residents around, plus millions of visitors every year, is an incredible feat.

London opened the world's first underground railway in 1863. It has one of the largest bus fleets in the world with over 9,000 buses on 675 routes. Plus, there is the Docklands Light Railway, National Rail services, the London Overground, river services, trams and taxis, which are all integral to London's transport needs.

London's public transport system is excellent and if you will be spending all your time in central London only (and using public transport), then the Oyster Card, Bus and Underground sections are must-reads.

The Oyster Card

What is an Oyster Card?
Introduced in 2003, the Oyster Card is a contactless rechargeable smartcard that you can use on London's public transport.

Although cash is still accepted of most services in London, over 95% of all journeys are made using a contactless payment method, such as the Oyster Card (note: cash is *not* accepted on London buses).

Oyster Cards eliminate the need to search for change when boarding public transport and speeds up journeys considerably.

The Oyster card has largely replaced the paper Travelcard (see the next section) for most Londoners. This is because it is faster, easier and cheaper than paper tickets.

Will it save me money?
An Oyster Card is a serious money saver, with big discounts over cash fares. As an example, a cash journey on the Underground in central London (zone 1) is £4.90 at any time of day.

The equivalent journey paid using an Oyster Card is £2.40. That's a saving of over 50%!

Where can I get one?
The easiest way to get an Oyster Card, is to visit any Underground station where Oyster Cards can be purchased from ticket machines directly. There is a £5 refundable deposit for the card. You can then top it up at the ticket machines at any station, online, at Customer Service locations, as well as at independent retailers showing Oyster advertising on shop windows. You can top-up your card using both cash or credit and debit cards.

You can also buy an Oyster Card at many newsagents throughout the city and visitor centres.

Once your visit to London has ended, you can choose to either keep your Oyster Card, or get a refund. Your refund will be for all the credit left on the card (up to £10), as well as the £5 deposit you paid for the card. You can do this at certain ticket machines at Underground stations. Avoid buying "Visitor Oyster cards".

How do I use an Oyster Card?
On a bus, you tap your Oyster Card on the yellow reader by the driver on the way in (see image). You do not need to do anything when leaving the bus as all bus journeys are a flat fare, regardless of distance.

On all rail services (including the Underground), you must tap your Oyster Card on the yellow reader on the way in (either at a ticket barrier or a standalone reader if there are no barriers), and also on the way out to calculate the correct fare. Failure to do so will result in a penalty charge. If you only tap in or out, but not both, you will be charged extra.

How much is a single journey on the tube with Oyster?
• Zone 1 Only – £2.40 always
• Zones 1 and 2 – £2.90 peak, £2.40 off-peak
• Zones 1 to 3 – £3.30 peak, £2.80 off-peak
• Zones 1 to 4 – £3.90 peak, £2.80 off-peak
• Zones 1 to 5 – £4.70 peak,

£3.10 off-peak
• Zones 1 to 6 – £5.10 peak, £3.10 off-peak

Peak times are 06:30 to 09:30 both into and out of central London, and 16:00 to 19:00 going from central London outwards.

Daily Capping
When you travel using an Oyster Card, the system automatically sets a daily "cap". When your total day's fares reach this amount, you are not charged further. This is the equivalent price of a 1-Day Travelcard, or less.

Daily caps on Oyster Cards:
• Zone 1 Only – £6.80

• Zone 1 and 2 – £6.80
• Zones 1 to 3 – £8.00
• Zones 1 to 4 – £9.80
• Zones 1 to 5 – £11.60
• Zones 1 to 6 – £12.50

If you plan to use your Oyster Card far at least 5 days out of 7, a 7-day Travelcard can be added to your Oyster Card to save money. See the next section.

By the end of 2018, it is expected that Oyster will also be able to apply a weekly cap from Monday to Sunday and not charge more than a 7-Day Travelcard.

Travelcards

A Travelcard is a 1-Day, 7-Day, 1-Month or annual ticket with unlimited travel on London Underground, buses, trams, National Rail services, the Overground and the DLR.

You can buy the Travelcard for the zones you want – if you will stay in central London, then a Zone 1 & 2 Travelcard is sufficient.

The 1-Day Travelcard is a paper ticket. 7-Day and longer Travelcards are added to an Oyster Card; they are not sold as paper.

A Travelcard runs for 7 consecutive days or 1 month from the start date – not a calendar week or a calendar month. For example, a 7-day travel starting on a Tuesday is valid until next Monday night. You choose the start date when purchasing.

The monthly Travelcard works similarly - it runs 1 full month from the start date, not a calendar month. E.g. If you buy a monthly travelcard from 17th March, it expires on 16th April at midnight.

If you'll make a single journey outside your Travelcard zones, add a few pounds credit to your Oyster Card and it will charge you the correct fare.

Travelcard Pricing
• Zone 1 to 2 – £12.70 per day, £34.10 for a week
• Zones 1 to 3 – £12.70 per day, £40.00 for a week
• Zones 1 to 4 – £12.70 per day, £49.00 for a week

Options are available for additional zones. Travelcards are sold at all Underground ticket machines.

Contactless Travel

The entire Underground, Bus, Overground, Tram, National Rail and DLR network are Contactless enabled. This means that you no longer need to buy an Oyster Card or paper ticket to travel.

You can tap your contactless-enabled debit or credit card (cards should display the wave symbol as seen here) on the yellow Oyster Card readers and it will work in the same way as an Oyster Card. There is no need to top up, and money is taken from your bank account at the end of the day.

International visitors should be aware that many banks charge fees for foreign transactions.

Contactless travel prices are the same as on an Oyster Card, and there is a daily cap as on Oyster. Contactless users also benefit from a weekly price cap (Monday to Sunday only) at the price as a 7-day Travelcard.

You cannot add a Travelcard

to a contactless payment card.

Apple Pay, Android Pay and Samsung Pay all also work the same way as a contactless payment card. Remember to have enough mobile phone battery to complete the journey.

Journey Planning

Modern technology makes it easier to travel around London than ever before.

Transport for London's website – tfl.gov.uk – allows you to plan a journey from any station, point of interest or postcode to another within London, giving you the best route options. You can also see live bus, train and tube departure times.

The website is optimised for mobile phones.

We, however, recommend using the smartphone app *Citymapper* – it has the same features as the TfL website, plus many more. It, allows you to plan journeys, see live transport departures, Santander Cycles bike availability, and includes tube and rail maps.

Our favourite *Citymapper* feature is the companion-style help every step of the way, even telling you when to get off a bus (using GPS), and automatically adjusting your estimated arrival time in real time. This app requires an active internet connection to plan journeys, but you can make your trip without a connection.

National Rail

If you plan on venturing outside London or to the suburbs, you may use National Rail trains. They are not operated by Transport for London like the rest of London's transport; each route is run by a different Train Operating Company.

You can buy a paper ticket, use an Oyster Card or Contactless payment to board National Rail services within London zones 1 to

9 (more on zones in our Underground section), and certain other stations. You can also use Oyster Cards and Contactless on National Rail services to and from Gatwick Airport, including the Gatwick Express.

Oyster Cards and Contactless payments are not valid on the Heathrow Express, and the Heathrow Connect between Hayes & Harlington and Heathrow

(but will be from May 2018).

They are also not accepted on East Midlands Trains, Grand Central, Hull Trains, Virgin Trains, or Virgin Trains East Coast services – these trains do not stop within London anyway, they are services to cities and towns outside the UK which start in London. For these journeys, standalone tickets are required.

London Underground

The London Underground (also known as the "tube") is the world's oldest underground railway system, having started operation in 1863.

The system has grown to 270 stations, 250 miles (402km), and on a busy day the tube carries over 4.8 million passengers. In central London, it is generally never more than a 10-minute walk to a station, making the Underground a great way to get around.

The Underground is made up of eleven lines; these connect with the Overground, TfL Rail, DLR National Rail and from late 2018, the Elizabeth Line.

The Underground is currently undergoing a huge refurbishment and upgrade program and all the trains and stations are being modernised.

How busy and safe is the tube?

At peak times, the Underground experiences heavy overcrowding and stations are sometimes temporarily closed in order to avoid the overloading of platforms. It is unlikely you can board a train at rush hour and find a seat. Standing room can be very limited too.

During off-peak times of the day, it is an entirely different experience and finding a seat is far from a challenge.

The Underground system is clean, efficient and safe - the Hammersmith and

City, District, Circle and Metropolitan lines have air-conditioned trains, but other lines do not.

Zones

The Underground, Overground, National Rail, TfL Rail, Elizabeth Line and Docklands Light Railway operate on Transport for London's zonal system. This categorises stations into zones depending on their distance from central London. Stations in the immediate centre are in Zone 1, those furthest away are in Zone 6.

The main zones are zones 1 to 6, with only a few stations in extended zones numbered 7 to 9. Zones are used to calculate fares. Travelling through more zones means a higher fare.

You only need to know your destination station name and staff can figure out what ticket you need, but if you purchase a Travelcard it is useful to know which zones you require. If you are using Oyster Pay as You Go, this is largely irrelevant to

you can just add credit ("top up") as required.

If you are visiting the city centre, you will probably not venture outside Zones 1 to 2. As a visitor you will rarely have to travel further than Zone 4.

Zones do NOT apply to buses: there is a flat fare.

Step-Free Accessibility

London underground is far from fully accessible due to the system's age. Advances are being made, but visitors with limited mobility should check before they travel for the best route as step-free access is still very limited - only 71 of the 270 offer step-free access.

Hours of Operation

Trains run on the underground at frequent intervals and it is uncommon to wait for a train in central London for more than 4 minutes. A wait of 1 to 2 minutes is typical. This makes it a very efficient way of getting around.

The Underground is not a

24-hour system. The first trains leave depots at about 5:00am, with the last trains returning at 1:00am. This allows for a 3- to 4-hour gap for maintenance work.

If you need an early or late train, particularly on a Sunday, check the timetables – on Sunday trains start up to 90 minutes later than on weekdays, and service ends about an hour earlier than other days.

Christmas Timetable

There are no Transport for London services on Christmas Day and services end early on Christmas eve. On the crossover from New Years Eve to New Years Day, the trains run all night long.

Night Tube

On Friday and Saturday, the tube offers a 24-hour service on the majority of the Central line and Piccadilly line, the Charing Cross branch of the Northern Line and all of the Victoria Line and Jubilee Line. A small part of the Overground joins in December 2017.

Trains run every 8 to 20 minutes, on the nights of Friday to Saturday, and Saturday to Sunday only.

Where's the tube map?

Due to licensing restrictions, fees and the ever-changing London Underground map, we cannot include the official map in this guide. We recommend you download the PDF map of the underground from bit.ly/lontubemap. This does not include National Rail services, but does include the Overground, TfL Rail/Elizabeth Line and the DLR.

We recommend you have this on a mobile phone or print it out. Free printed maps are available at all Underground stations.

Phone Signal & Wi-Fi

There is no phone signal when underground, though this is set to arrive in late 2018. Most Underground stations, including entrance halls, platforms and escalators have high-speed Wi-Fi access. There is no Wi-Fi onboard Underground trains themselves or in the tunnels between stations.

Customers of Virgin Media, EE, Three, O2 and Vodafone get free access to this Wi-Fi. Other passengers may purchase a Wi-Fi pass access directly on their device by connecting to the network. The fee is £2 for a day, £5 for a week or £15 for a month.

All passengers can see the status of the tube lines on their smartphone without having to buy a Wi-Fi pass.

Elizabeth Line (starts December 2018)

A huge new underground rail line that is opening in phases from December 2018 to December 2019. In total it will add 10% more rail capacity to the capital and dramatically speed up journeys. The Elizabeth Line will link east and west London, as well as commuting towns outside the city.

Ticketing works in the same way as on the Underground (Oyster, Contactless and paper tickets) and stations will be integrated with the Underground and Overground networks. The Elizabeth Line will also be featured on tube map.

Travellers from Heathrow Airport will be particularly pleased to hear that the line will stop at all terminals, with up to 6 trains per hour, connecting Heathrow to many places in central London and drastically reducing journey times. Heathrow Terminal 2 & 3 to Bond Street will only take 26 minutes.

From December 2018 to May 2019, you will need to change trains at Paddington to go to and from Heathrow. From May 2019, direct services will run.

The line will also allow journeys within central

London to be made more quickly.

Trains will run every 2.5 minutes at rush hour, carry up to 1500 passengers each and feature air conditioning. Stations will be modern and more spacious compared to the underground.

Buses

Buses are a fantastic way to get around London. They are clean, efficient, and are fully accessible to wheelchair users, and include audio and visual announcements too. Plus, with dedicated bus lanes in many cases a journey on a bus is quicker than the equivalent journey by car.

Buses in London are cashless – you must use either an Oyster Card or contactless payment to board. A paper Day Travelcard or Day Bus & Tram Pass can also be used on board buses and is sold at tube station ticket machines.

The fare for one journey is £1.50. A paper One-Day Bus & Tram pass is £5, however if you use Contactless or Oyster Pay as You Go, then the maximum you will pay per day is £4.50, making this better value than the paper bus day pass. If you run out of money on your Oyster Card, you can make "one more journey" and your card will dip into a negative balance. A receipt will be printed to alert you of this. The negative balance must be repaid next time when topping up or you cannot make further journeys.

For those on a budget, the £4.50 price cap for bus-only travel on Oyster Cards offers fantastic value for money. As buses do not have zones, you can travel (slowly) all over London for this price.

You can make a second bus journey within 1 hour on any route and this journey will be free. From Spring 2018, you should be able to make unlimited bus journeys within 1 hour for just £1.50.

You can check the time of your next bus either through electronic 'countdown' signs at some bus stops, or by following the text message instructions posted at bus stops. Printed timetables and schedules are also available at bus stops.

Most bus routes in central London have a bus every 10 minutes or more frequently; on Sundays, this wait increases to 'up to' every 20 minutes.

The section below lists some of the most notable locations on central London's key bus routes. Grab a seat up top and make your own bus tour.

Key Central London Bus Routes:

- **Route 8** – Shoreditch High Street, Liverpool Street, Bank, Holborn and Tottenham Court Road
- **Route 9** – Aldwych, Trafalgar Square, St. James's Palace, Green Park, Knightsbridge, and High Street Kensington
- **Route 10** – King's Cross, St Pancras, Euston, Tottenham Court Road, Oxford Street, Bond Street, Marble Arch, Knightsbridge and High Street Kensington
- **Route 11** – Liverpool Street, Bank, St Paul's Cathedral, Fleet Street, Trafalgar Square, Westminster, Victoria and Sloane Square
- **Route 14** – Euston Square, Tottenham Court Road, Piccadilly Circus, Green Park, Knightsbridge and South Kensington
- **Route 15** – Aldgate, Tower of London, Monument, St Paul's Cathedral, Fleet Street and Trafalgar Square
- **Route 23** – Strand, Trafalgar Square, Piccadilly Circus, Oxford Circus, Bond Street, Marble Arch, Edgware Road and Paddington
- **Route 24** – Camden Town, Euston Square, Tottenham Court Road, Leicester Square, Trafalgar Square and Westminster

- **Route 38** – British Museum, Piccadilly Circus, Green Park, Hyde Park Corner and Victoria
- **Route 59** – St Pancras, Russell Square, Aldwych, Waterloo and Imperial War Museum
- **Route 73** – Kings Cross, St Pancras, Euston, Tottenham Court Road and Oxford Circus
- **Route 74** – South Kensington, Knightsbridge, Park Lane, Marble Arch and Baker Street

- **Route 139** – Abbey Road, Baker Street, Oxford Circus, Piccadilly Circus, Trafalgar Square and Waterloo
- **Route 274** – Lancaster Gate, Marble Arch, Baker Street, Camden Town, London Zoo and Lord's Cricket Ground
- **Route C2** – Regent Street, Oxford Street, London Zoo and Camden Town
- **Route RV1** – Covent Garden, Aldwych, Waterloo, London Eye, Tate Modern, London Bridge, Tower

Bridge and Tower of London

Transport for London has these key routes, and others, as a map for download at bit.ly/londbus.

Bus routes are always changing and there will be many alterations to routes from Summer 2018 onwards when a large part of Oxford Street is pedestrianised. More changes will come in December 2018 when the Elizabeth line opens.

London Overground and Docklands Light Railway (DLR)

London Overground

The Overground works in a very similar manner to the Underground. Its routes are featured on the tube map and should be treated the same as any underground line, except that these run above the surface. Most visitors to London will not use the Overground as it is mainly an orbital railway linking London's suburbs.

Docklands Light Railway

The Docklands Light Railway is a light rail system connecting east and central London. DLR trains are driverless and computer operated and provide great views of the Canary Wharf financial district along the way. You may encounter the DLR if you are visiting Stratford (for the Olympic Park), Greenwich (for the Cutty Sark, the naval museums and the observatory), Bank and Tower Hill (for the Tower of London).

Oyster Cards, contactless payments and paper tickets

work on the Overground and DLR as on the Underground. Be aware that on both the Overground and the DLR, many stations do not have ticket barriers and instead have standalone card readers on the platforms or by station entrances – remember to tap your Oyster Card or contactless payment at these before boarding a train to pay the correct fare.

Step Free Accessibility:

57 of the 112 Overground stations offer step-free access. All DLR stations offer step-free access from the street to the train.

Wi-Fi on the Overground

Over 70 Overground stations provide Wi-Fi access. Wi-Fi is not available on the trains, but at the stations themselves. Access is free to everyone, provided by The Cloud. Wi-Fi is not available on the DLR. The majority of the DLR and Overground is above ground with good phone and data signal.

Nighttime services:
Like some lines on the Underground, a small section of the Overground runs throughout the night on the nights from Friday to Saturday and Saturday to Sunday. From December 2017, the Overground will run from Dalston Junction in east London to New Cross Gate in south east London.

From 2018, the night Overground will also run to Canonbury and Highbury & Islington in east London.

Trains will not stop at Whitechapel station until December 2018.

There is no public date for a nighttime service on the DLR.

River Services

There are two types of Thames river services in London - scenic sightseeing river cruises (with commentary), and river taxi services (no commentary).

Thames Clippers runs the river taxi services in London. Five routes currently run; the most commonly used route for visitors is RB1 which links the London Eye eastwards towards Embankment, Blackfriars, London Bridge, Tower Bridge, Canary Wharf, Greenwich and North Greenwich (for *The O2*).

River services operate every 20 to 30 minutes on all lines, and the boats have onboard cafés, bars and seating. Most boats also have onboard toilets. Journeys take about 17 minutes from the London Eye to Tower Pier, and 45 minutes from the London Eye to The O2. All passengers are guaranteed a seat by law.

Pricing

Fares for river services are expensive compared to the rest of London's transport network. If you buy your tickets at ticket offices, adult single fares vary between £4.40 and £9 depending on the distance travelled. A River Roamer day ticket (unlimited travel in Central and East areas from 9:00am) is £18.50. Children 5 to 15 pay half price. Under 5s travel free.

If you buy your ticket online, use an Oyster Card (Pay as You Go), contactless payment, or on the Thames Clipper app, prices are

cheaper - £3.90 to £7.20 for a single ticket, and £16.30 for a River Roamer (online only).

Travelcards are not valid on river services but you will receive a 33% discount off your river ticket or pass.

Top Tip: These are commuter boats with no commentary. However, Thames Clipper has created an audio guide for your journey that works using the GPS on your phone. The app is called "Thames Clippers in:flow", and is available on Apple and Android devices.

Tramlink

If you venture into South London, towards Wimbledon, for example, you may come across London Tramlink – a tram system.

The system is designed for local residents more than visitors in reality, and travels through some of the suburbs of south London.

The tram system functions in much the same way as

buses do in London.

The fare is £1.50 with an Oyster Card or contactless payment. The drivers of the trams do not sell tickets onboard like buses.

You must touch in your Oyster Card or contactless payment card at one of the readers before boarding the tram – do not touch out when you leave, except at Wimbledon where you must

touch out to get through the ticket barriers.

The daily price cap is £4.50 if using Oyster. A One Day Bus & Tram Pass can also be purchased for £5.

If you have a Travelcard on your Oyster card or a paper Day Travelcard that includes Zone 3, 4, 5 or 6, you can use it to travel on all trams.

Cycling

One of the cheapest and best ways to get around London is by bike. Cycling has become a huge phenomenon in London over the past 10 years, and many commuters now use it as their main form of travel.

Cycling is allowed on all roads unless stated otherwise. You may not ride on the pavement, and some parks have specially designated cycle lanes – you must not ride outside these lanes. In the UK, wearing a helmet is not legally required but we strongly recommend it.

SANTANDER CYCLES

London's public bike hire scheme is Santander Cycles. The bikes are also commonly called 'Boris Bikes' after the then Mayor of London, Boris Johnson, who introduced for the scheme.

The scheme has 10,000 bicycles for hire and there are 700 docking stations, each with many spaces to get or drop off a bike.

You simply walk up to any cycle docking station with an available bike (located every 300m to 500m), insert your credit or debit card into the payment terminal and select the number of bikes you would like to hire.

Your receipt will contain a code; tap this into one of the keypads next to the bikes and it will be released. Ride and then return the bike to any docking point around the city.

The scheme offers good value for money for those who use it right. Fees are split into two parts: an access charge and a journey charge.

The daily access price is £2 for a 24-hour pass. The access charge allows you to make as many journeys as you wish, each lasting 30 minutes or less, during the 24-hour period with no extra fee to pay. If you make a journey over 30 minutes, there is a journey charge of £2 per 30 minutes.

The idea is that you use the bike to go between places and not to continuously ride around all day. This ensures that there are always bikes in circulation.

If you have a single journey that is longer than 30 minutes (unlikely if you are just sightseeing), then you can split your journey before you get to the 30-minute mark and wait 5 minutes between hires to avoid this extra charge.

When returning a bike, if you reach a docking station with no free bike spaces, simply go to the terminal at the docking station and tap the button that says "No docking point free". Follow the on-screen instructions. This will tell you where there are free spaces nearby, and grant you 15 extra minutes to return your bike.

For visitors to the city who want to keep fit and save money, while also getting around relatively quickly, this scheme is perfect.

The bikes are available 24 hours a day, 7 days a week. Get the official smartphone app to see the availability and location of docking stations updated in real time or use another app like *Citymapper* which we recommended earlier in this section.

CYCLE LANES AND CYCLE SUPERHIGHWAYS

As cycling has become so popular in recent years, cycle lanes have become increasingly common in London, particularly in the central area.

When a cycle lane is available, cyclists should stick to it, as it is usually the safest option.

Cycle lanes are commonly located next to bus lanes, and cyclists should be particularly wary of left-turning traffic when riding.

The city is also building and upgrading London Cycle Superhighways. Older versions share the road space with existing vehicles with a bike lane painted onto the road; newer Superhighways are completely segregated from traffic with a dedicated cycling area. These separated schemes make cycling in these areas much safer and more pleasant.

One of the best Superhighways stretches runs from Tower of London past Big Ben, Buckingham Palace and through Hyde Park.

Emirates Air Line

The Emirates Air Line is a cable car system in East London with views of the surrounding area, as well as a link between North Greenwich (for the O2 Arena) and Royal Victoria station on the DLR.

It is a unique way to see London but we wouldn't make a special trip to the area just to ride it. The Air Line is subject to weather conditions.

Crossings take 5 minutes during the rush hour peak of 7:00 to 9:00, 10 minutes from 9:00 to 19:00, and Night Flights are 12 to 13 minutes after 19:00. Cabins arrive every 15 to 30 seconds with room for 10 people.

The Air Line begins operation at 07:00 Monday to Friday, 08:00 on Saturday and 09:00 on Sunday. Closing times are 21:00 daily, except Friday and Saturday when it closes at

23:00. During Summer (April to September) closing times may be extended.

Fares are £4.50 for a single journey if paid by cash, and £3.50 if paid using an Oyster Card with Pay as You Go credit, or contactless.

Return fares are double the single fare. Child fares are half price. Pay as You Go fares do not count towards the Oyster daily cap.

For a more serene return

journey, the Discovery Experience includes in-flight audio and video, a souvenir guide and entrance to the nearby Emirates Aviation Experience. The Discovery Experience is priced at £10.70 for adults (cash) or £8.40 (Oyster and contactless); child prices are £6.20 and £5.00 respectively.

Night Flights (after 19:00) with on-board music and video are the same price as a standard daytime ticket.

Taxis

Taxis are a popular way to get around the capital and in many cases can be the quickest and most comfortable journey from A-to-B within London.

Taxis (Black Cabs) can use many bus lanes, making journeys quicker than driving your own car. Plus, no parking, Congestion Charge or fuel costs.

How do I hail a cab?
Black cabs are available to hail in London by sticking your arm out near the road. Do not shout out 'Taxi'. You should only hail cabs that have the "Taxi" light switched on as these are available. Those with the light switched off are unavailable for hire.

You can also find cabs at taxi ranks throughout the city – these are common at airports and rail stations.

Black cabs can also be pre-booked in advance through one of many taxi firms. Well known firms include Dial-a-Cab (0207 253 5000) and Radio Taxis (0207 272 0272), but many others are also available.

Finally, the technological elite may prefer to book a black cab through an app – myTaxi and Gett are the biggest ones out there. This is cashless and you can guarantee a cab, pre-book and see the price up-front.

Use promo code "giovanni.dac" for £10 off your first ride with myTaxi. With Gett, the discount code is "GTWVOHC". You can add these promo codes on the apps' setting screens.

What training do cab drivers go through?
Cab drivers go through a rigorous test called 'The Knowledge'. They must learn over 25,000 streets within 6 miles (10km) of Charing Cross in central London – and the quickest way to get you there. Most people take three years to pass this test. Generally speaking, cab drivers are friendly and happy to help you with questions.

How much do London cabs cost?
Transport for London sets the pricing for all taxis. Below is their pricing grid:

Distance	Approx journey time	Monday to Friday 05:00 - 20:00 (Tariff 1)	Monday to Friday 20:00 - 22:00 Saturday and Sunday 05:00 - 22:00 (Tariff 2)	Every night 22:00 - 05:00 Public holidays (Tariff 3)
1 mile	6 - 13 mins	£6 - £9.40	£6 - £9.40	£7 - £9.20
2 miles	10 - 20 mins	£9 - £14.60	£9.60 - £14.80	£10.60 - £15
4 miles	16 - 30 mins	£16 - £23	£17 - £23	£18 - £28
6 miles	28 - 40 mins	£24 - £31	£30 - £33	£29 - £34
Between Heathrow and Central London	30 - 60 mins	£48 - £90	£48 - £90	£48 - £90

Taxi journeys are priced using a mixture of journey length and journey time. The minimum fare is £2.60.

Passengers pay the metered fare, unless a set fare has been agreed at the start of the journey – set fares are rare in London cabs. As far as tipping is concerned, rounding to the nearest £1 or £5 is common practice.

All taxis accept cash, debit and credit card, and contactless payments.

There is no surcharge for card payments.

Driving

Roads in London can be cumbersome to drive on. Many are in a bad state and drivers from other cities may be surprised at how narrow some roads are. There is no simple road system either – London expanded from a series of villages to a huge city with no grid-based system like New York City. Therefore, a GPS system and/or a map is highly recommended.

Driving laws in the UK may differ from elsewhere, so do research these thoroughly before arrival.

The Congestion Charge
London's traffic reduction method is called the Congestion Charge (CC) and is on vehicles entering central London. The money from this charge funds improvements to the road and public transport system. Some vehicles are exempt.

The charge is £11.50 per day between the hours of 7am and 6pm, Monday to Friday. The Congestion Charge area applies to much of central London, and almost all the main attractions in London are inside the charging area. Before reaching an area that is subject to the Congestion Charge, road signs will warn you and indicate how to avoid it well in advance.

You have until midnight to pay your CC online; you can also pay the next day, when the charge increases to £14. If you fail to pay the charge, you will be fined (£65 to £130). If you are in a rental car, the rules also apply to you.

The T-Charge
Introduced in November 2017, the T-Charge aims to reduce car-based emissions in London by charging vehicles which do not meet minimum emission standards an additional £10 per day on top of the CC.

The T-Charge applies at the same times of the day as the CC. Cars that do not meet standards are broadly from 2005 or earlier, but it is worth checking your specific vehicle on tfl.gov.uk.

Filling Up
The place where you get your fuel from - usual petrol or diesel is called a "petrol station" - in the UK. Be sure to know which fuel your car takes. Petrol stations are few and far between in central London and queues can be long at each one. Major petrol stations in central London include:

• Esso – 115 Maida Vale, W9 1UP. Open 24/7.
• Esso – 393 Edgware Road, W2 1BT. Open 24/7.
• Esso – 77 Park Lane, W1K 7HB
• Shell – 106 Old Brompton Road, SW7 3RA
• BP – 238 Kennington Lane, SE11 5RD. Open 24/7

• Texaco – 212 Kennington Road, SE11 6PR

Parking
Parking in central London can be difficult (and expensive), so we recommend locating car parks closest to your destination before setting off. Local road signs can help in some areas.

Parking can be "pay and display" or "phone parking". In some areas you must pay for parking in advance. Breaking parking rules attracts a Penalty Charge Notice (PCN) and, in certain areas, your car may be clamped and towed. These range from £80 to £130 depending on the offence.

Some large shopping centres and shops have their own private parking which may or may not charge a fee.

Parking charges in central London differ on weekdays and weekends. Charges vary but can be up to £10 per hour in central London. Saturday prices are generally cheaper, and on Sundays some areas offer free parking.

Top 10 Must-See Attractions

❶ Tower of London

The Tower of London is undoubtedly our favourite major sight. It is amazing to see this castle, constructed in 1078, still standing in the very heart of London today.

Enjoy tours held by the Yeoman Warders or 'Beefeaters', walk across the castle's walls, see the Crown Jewels up close, and learn about the gruesome history of the Tower from executions to traitors. Allow at least three to four hours for a good overview.

❷ Houses of Parliament and Big Ben

Home of the UK government for over 500 years, the Houses of Parliament are world-renowned. The current building dates from the 1840s. The most famous part of the building is undoubtedly the clock tower which lies on its northern side, largely referred to as Big Ben.

Paid tours of the inside of the building are available and advanced reservations are strongly recommended

❸ Hyde Park and Kensington Gardens

Once Henry VIII's hunting grounds, today these two green areas combine to make a royal park spanning 625 acres.

Admire the Serpentine lake, the Princess Diana Memorial Fountain, and the Italian Gardens and Fountains. The Serpentine Galleries are also free of charge. Plus, see Speakers' Corner near Marble Arch where you can see people exercising their right of free speech.

❹ Natural History Museum

The Natural History Museum is one of London's most popular and beloved institutions, featuring a wide variety of permanent exhibitions in its collection.

Learn about the forces that shape our planet such as volcanoes and earthquakes, see how humans have evolved and witness how amazingly diverse life is on Earth. See birds, insects, fossils and more, and enjoy watching scientists at work at the Darwin Centre.

❺ Science Museum

Learn about outer space and moon landings, take part in interactive exhibitions, marvel at the history of flight, see how steam trains revolutionised the world in the Energy Hall, and more. A whole area dedicated to young children with shows and interactive exhibitions means that learning can be fun.

You can also find an IMAX screen showing scientific movies, as well as a simulator attraction and numerous kids play areas to show younger visitors how fun and interesting science can be.

❻ London Eye

For a unique view of London, step into one of the magnificent viewing capsules on the London Eye. It is the world's tallest cantilevered Ferris wheel and from the top, you can see up to 40km on a clear day.

The London Eye is constantly rotating and a journey onboard lasts 30 minutes. As you travel, you can gaze across London, have a quick break on the seats in the middle of the capsule, or use the onboard tablets to learn about the monuments around you.

❻ Trafalgar Square and National Gallery

Trafalgar Square is a magnificent space that celebrates Lord Nelson's victory in 1805 against the French and Spanish forces. Nelson's Column dominates the square, standing at 135 feet tall. Atop the column is a statue of Nelson himself.

The National Gallery here is free admission and houses priceless works of art including Van Gogh's 'Sunflowers' and Monet's 'Water Lillies' The works of art on offer cover several centuries, and even the building's interior architecture is worth admiring.

❽ British Museum

The British Museum is one of the largest museums in the world and houses over seven million artefacts relating to human history and culture.

Perhaps the most famous item on display is the Rosetta Stone, which was the key to us understanding Egyptian hieroglyphics. The cat mummies are also fascinating, as are the Egyptian sarcophagi, also on display, and the ancient Greek temples.

❾ The West End: Piccadilly Circus & Leicester Square

The West End is one of the busiest and liveliest areas of London. Piccadilly Circus anchors one side of the West End with the famous Piccadilly Lights, the giant advertising billboards. The first of these was put up back in 1908, and was the world's first set of outdoor electric lights.

In Leicester Square, you can enjoy the multitude of souvenir shops, as well as the cinemas where film premieres are regularly held. Street performers also often conduct shows in this area.

❿ Buckingham Palace

Home of the monarch since Queen Victoria made it her residence in 1837, Buckingham Palace has become a true icon of London. From the famous balcony to the iconic guards and the golden Victoria statue and fountain, Buckingham Palace is a sight not to be missed.

For most of the year, the public are not allowed inside the palace. However, a summer opening does allow visitors for a limited period of time into the State Rooms and palace gardens.

The Changing the Guard ceremony takes at the front of the palace.

Chapter Six

Neighbourhood Guides

In this section, we have split central London into areas and cover things to see, dining and accommodation options.

Below is a very simple diagram of where these different areas are located in central London.

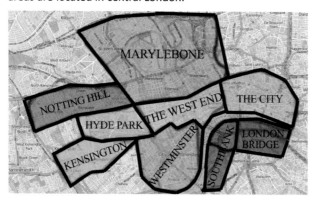

Each area is unique in character; from areas filled with galleries and theatres, to residential areas.

We highly recommend you bookmark attractions you would like to see and the restaurants you would like to eat in. We also list accommodation options allowing you to choose somewhere that fits your taste and budget best.

Concession prices listed usually apply to over 60s or over 65s (proof may be requested), and students on production of a valid student ID. Child ages vary wildly by attraction. Some museums may list two prices: one with an optional donation and one without - you can choose which price to pay. Please also note most attractions are closed between 24 and 26 December.

To ease your planning, each listing includes information along with symbols. These are easy to understand but we include the following key for your reference.

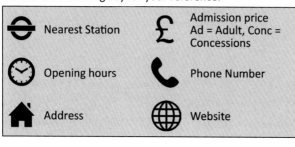

Westminster, Victoria & St. James's

Westminster is well known for being the home of the UK government, with the Houses of Parliament being where debates are held. Westminster Abbey and Buckingham Palace show that state, church and royalty mix together well in this area of London.

See and Do

The Queen's Gallery

 St. James's Park and Victoria

 Ad: £11, Ages 5 to 17: £5.50, Conc: £9.20

 Daily 10:00 to 17:30. From 21 July 2018 to 30 Sep 2018, gallery hours are 9:30 to 17:30. Closed 13 Nov to 7 Dec 2017. Closed 25 and 26 Dec yearly.

 Buckingham Palace Rd, SW1A 1AA

 royalcollection.org.uk

This gallery showcases a constantly rotating series of works from the Royal Collection.

Over 450 works can be seen at any one time.

Be sure to check for what the latest exhibition is before visiting.

Tickets for this attraction can be combined with those for The Royal Mews and even Buckingham Palace's State Room tours (summer only) for savings.

Clarence House

 Green Park and Charing Cross

 Adults and Concessions – £10.30, Children (5 to 16) – £6.20

 Open 1st to 31st August 2018. Mon to Fri 10:00 to 16:30, Sat and Sun 10:00 to 17:30.

 Little St James's Street, St. James's, SW1A 1BA

 royalcollection.org.uk

Clarence House is the official London residence of Prince Charles (The Prince of Wales), and Camilla (The Duchess of Cornwall). The building was designed by John Nash and was completed in 1827, and is located right next door to St. James's Palace. The house was the residence of Queen Elizabeth, The Queen Mother.

The house is open daily to visitors via guided tours in August each year.

Buckingham Palace

 St. James's Park and Victoria

 Ad: £24, Ages 5 to 17: £13.50, Conc: £22

 21 July 2018 to 30 September 2018.

 royalcollection .org.uk

 Buckingham Palace Rd, SW1A 1AA

Home of the monarch since Queen Victoria made it her home in 1837, Buckingham Palace has become a true icon of London. From the famous balcony to the iconic guards, and the golden Victoria memorial statue to the imposing fountain, Buckingham Palace is a sight not to be missed.

The 'Changing the Guard' ceremony is one of the main attractions of the palace where you can see the royal guards marching to the palace to replace another regiment, accompanied by a band. The guard change ceremony happens daily in the summer (usually April to July) and on Monday, Wednesday, Friday and Sunday during the rest of

the year. Check online to confirm dates for your visit as these are frequently affected by events, especially around Christmas and New Year.

The ceremony reaches its height at around 11:00am at Buckingham Palace, but you want to be there at least 45 minutes before for a good spot.

Access inside the palace is strictly restricted. For most of the year you cannot go inside Buckingham Palace itself, but can instead visit The Royal Mews and The Queen's Gallery throughout the year.

During Winter, usually from mid-December to late-January, there are

exclusive 2.5-hour guided tours available to reserve. The latest iteration run from 15th December 2017 to 4th February 2018. Tours are £80 per person.

Furthermore, during the Summer, the nineteen State Rooms of the palace are available to visit, as well as the gardens in a self-guided tour. A visit to the State Rooms will last about two hours total once you are inside. In 2018, the State Rooms are open from 21 July 2018 to 30 September 2018.

The State Rooms tour is one of our favourite things to do in all of London and comes highly recommended.

The Royal Mews

 St. James's Park and Victoria

 Ad: £10, Under 17: £5.80, Conc: £9.20

 Daily 10:00 to 17:00 Apr to Oct, Mon to Sat 10:00 to 16:00 Feb, Mar & Nov. Closed Dec & Jan.

 royalcollection. org.uk

 Buckingham Palace Rd, SW1A 1AA

Located in Buckingham Palace's grounds, and open for the majority of the year, the Royal Mews is a working stable where you can see traditional coaches and carriages used in royal ceremonial occasions, as well as the horses themselves. The Diamond Jubilee State Coach on display is particularly stunning.

Furthermore, between April and October a 45-minute guided tour is available, and included in the price of your ticket. This showcases the highlights of the Royal Mews and is led by one of Buckingham Palace's wardens.

St. James's Palace

 Green Park

 Not open to the public.

 Not open to the public.

 royal.gov.uk

 Marlborough Rd, SW1A 1BS

St James's Palace was largely built during the 1530s, under the reign of Henry VIII, and has been home to monarchs for over 300 years.

Interestingly, despite the fact that all monarchs since Queen Victoria have lived at Buckingham Palace, St. James's is still the monarch's official residence.

Today the palace is used primarily for charity events where members of the royal family are often present, as well as offices for many royal functions.

The palace also contains the London residences of The Prince of Wales, The Princess Royal and Princess Alexandra.

Although the palace is not to visitors, it is still worth walking around the outside, particularly as it is located just down the road from Buckingham Palace.

Houses of Parliament & Big Ben

 Westminster

 Ad: £28, Age 5-15: £12, Conc: £23

 Sat all year. Most weekdays when parliament is not in session.

 www.parliament.uk/visiting/

 Parliament Square, SW1A 0AA

As home of the UK government for over 500 years, the Houses of Parliament are world-renowned. The current building dates from the 1840s when the previous building on the site was destroyed by a large fire in 1834 – only a small part remains. The Palace of Westminster that stood on this site was also destroyed by a fire in 1512.

The most famous part of the building is undoubtedly the clock tower which lies on its northern side, largely referred to as Big Ben. However, Big Ben is actually the name of the 13.5-ton bell located inside the Elizabeth Tower. The reason behind the bell's naming is still disputed to this day, but one likely reason is that Benjamin Hall was the commissioner of works at the time the original bell was installed.

Paid tours of the inside of the building are available and advanced reservations are strongly recommended. Tours are available on Saturdays year-round, except when Parliament is in recess - at these times, Parliament is open on weekdays.

The best place to check for exact opening dates and times is at parliament.uk/visiting/visiting-and-tours/tours-of-parliament/.

Guided tours last approximately 90 minutes. Live English tours depart every 15 to 20 minutes from 09:00 to 16:15. Audio tours are also available on the same dates and are self-guided.

Tours will take you inside the beautiful Westminster Hall, the Queen's Robing Room, the Royal Gallery, the Lords and Commons Chamber, St. Stephen's Hall and many more locations. Learn about the fascinating history, as well as how the building is used as a working location today.

Audio Tour prices are: Adults – £20.50, Child – £8.50 (one free child per paying adult), Concessions – £16. Discounts are available for pre-booking.

UK visitors may contact their local MP, or a member of the House of Lords, to request a free guided tour year-round. UK visitor tours last 75 minutes and these are generally fully booked 6 months in advance.

In addition, UK residents can tour the Elizabeth Tower and see Big Ben (the bell) up close by applying through the aforementioned methods – these tours are very popular and are also generally booked 6 months in advance.

The Houses of Parliament have become a trademark symbol for London and are daily staples in films, TV shows, documentaries and news programmes across the world.

Important: Big Ben's clock tower is currently undergoing a major refurbishment until 2021. During this time, the tower will be under scaffolding and the bells will be silenced. The remainder of the Houses of Parliament will also be undergoing a large refurbishment.

The Jewel Tower

 Westminster

 Ad: £5.50, Age 5-15: £3.30, Conc: £5

 Nov to Mar: weekends 10:00 to 16:00. Apr to Oct: Daily 10:00 to 17:40

 english-heritage.org.uk

 Abingdon Street, SW1P 3JX

Built in 1365 to house Edward III's personal treasure collection, the Jewel Tower is one of the few surviving areas of the old Palace of Westminster, which was razed by a fire. Today, you can find an exhibition that spans all three floors inside and revisits the tower's numerous roles over the past 650 years, and even includes a model of the Palace of Westminster before the 1834 fire destroyed it.

The Cenotaph

The nation's main war memorial, The Cenotaph is planted in the middle of the road in Whitehall. Flags of the United Kingdom are placed around the memorial.

This is also where the monarch and other senior members of the royal family, as well as politicians, lay wreaths of flowers every year in a large ceremony on Remembrance Sunday (the second Sunday in November).

 Westminster   Whitehall, SW1A 2AX   24/7 - Public area

Horse Guards Parade and The HouseHold Cavalry Museum

 Charing Cross and Westminster

 Museum - Ad: £7, Age 5-16 and Conc: £5

 10:00 to 17:00 Nov to Mar, late closing at 18:00 from Apr to Oct.

 householdcavalry museum.co.uk

 Whitehall, SW1A 2AX

Horse Guards Parade is a parade ground situated off Whitehall where you can see the Horse Guards (Household Cavalry) on duty daily from 10:00 to 16:00, guarding one of the official entrances to Buckingham Palace.

At 4:00pm every day, there is the inspection and dismount ceremony, that visitors can watch free of charge; simply turn up. The Changing of the Queen's Life Guard also takes place daily on Horse Guards Parade at 11:00am (10:00am on Sundays).

This parade ground also hosts "Trooping the Colour", an annual ceremony that is conducted on the monarch's official birthday in June.

The "Beating Retreat" is another ceremony held here on two successive evenings in June.

The parade ground, which today is accessible at all times, was formerly the venue of tournaments that were conducted during the reign of Henry VIII.

It was once also the headquarters of the British Army and home to the Duke of Wellington. Currently it houses the General Officer commanding the district of London in the British Army.

The Horse Guard Parade grounds are free to visit, but the museum is paid entry. Opening dates and prices listed are for the museum.

At the museum, visitors can appreciate the work that goes into being the Queen's mounted bodyguard with a unique behind the scenes look. A multi-language self-guided multimedia tour is offered to each guest at the museum and brings the exhibits to life, as you learn about this regiment's past and present.

Downing Street

 Green Park   Downing St, SW1A 2AA   Not open to the public. Visible from a distance 24/7.

Downing Street is the heart of Government, with number 10 being the most famous address – the Prime Minster's Office and Official Residence.

Number 11 is the residence of the Chancellor of the Exchequer, who manages the country's finances.

The origin of the street's name comes from when it was commissioned by Sir George Downing in the 1680s on the site of Hampden House.

Downing Street is not publicly accessible and is guarded by black gates and barriers, as well as armed police officers. You may take photos from Whitehall looking into Downing Street but cannot go any closer.

Westminster Abbey

 Westminster

 Ad: £22, Age 6-16: £10, Conc: £18

 Mon to Fri 9:30 to 15:30. Sat 9:30 to 13:30. Closed Sundays and religious holidays.

 westminster-abbey.org

 20 Deans Yard, SW1P 3PA

This construction of Westminster Abbey began in 1245, but previous incarnations of the church have existed on the site since 960. Over the years, several extensions were added, eventually finishing in its present form 500 later in 1745 with the West towers.

Westminster Abbey has been home to coronations since 1066 when William the Conqueror was crowned at the site. It has also been home to no less than eleven royal weddings, including most recently Prince William and Catherine Middleton in 2011.

Inside, the abbey is a magnificent work of art and the cloisters are equally worth a visit. Significant areas include the North Transept, the Sanctuary, the College Garden, the Tomb of Mary (Queen of Scotts), and Poet's Corner.

Be sure to look out for the Coronation Chair that has been in use since Edward II in 1308.

Guided tours of the inside of the Abbey are available for £5 extra per person and last about 90 minutes Multi-language audio tours are complimentary and available at the abbey entrance – alternatively there is app you can download on your smartphone.

The opening hours listed above are for visitors to the abbey. Services are free to all. On religious days such as Sunday, the Abbey is only open for services and not for visiting.

Most visitors will spend 90 minutes to 2 hours inside. Queues are lengthy for the abbey almost year-round.

2018 is an exciting year for the abbey as The Queen's Diamond Jubilee Galleries area set to open providing access to a part of the church which has been closed to the public for 700 years. The new galleries will give visitors magnificent views to the Palace of Westminster and into the church, displaying treasures and collections reflecting the Abbey's rich and varied thousand-year history.

Tate Britain

 Pimlico

 Free. Some temporary exhibitions have a fee.

 Daily 10:00 to 18:00.

 tate.org.uk/visit/tate-britain

 Millbank, SW1P 4RG

The Tate Britain houses a large collection of British art, including works from John Latham and Douglas Gordon.

The gallery also contains the largest number of works by J.M.W. Turner in the world.

Some of our favourite pieces include "King and Queen", a bronze sculpture by Henry Moore, and the stunning "Flatford Mill ('Scene on a Navigable River')" by John Constable.

Best of all - the museum charges no admission fee.

Free guided tours are offered throughout the day and last 45 minutes. Other complimentary tours and talks are also regularly held.

You can take advantage of the Tate-to-Tate riverboat service to travel to the Tate Modern on the Southbank if you are visiting both these museums on the same day. This is a paid riverboat service.

Churchill War Rooms

 Westminster

 Ad: £19, Age 5-15: £9.50, Conc: £15.20

 Daily 09:30 to 18:00

 iwm.org.uk/visits/churchill-war-rooms

 Clive Steps, King Charles Street, SW1A 2AQ

A fascinating museum located underground in the heart of Westminster. The war rooms were used by the government and Winston Churchill during the WW II. There are living quarters, planning rooms and even the original map room, which has been left unchanged since the war ended in 1945. It is a fascinating slice of London's history and a must-visit location for history lovers.

Banqueting House

 Westminster and Charing Cross

 Ad: £8, Under 16: Free, Conc.: £7

 Daily 10:00 to 17:00.

 hrp.org.uk

 Whitehall, SW1A 2AX

Banqueting House is the only surviving part of the old Whitehall Palace that once spanned the length of the road now called Whitehall. Almost all of Whitehall Palace burnt down in a 1698 fire; only Banqueting House remains.

From the art and sculptures, to the stunning interiors, and even the site of King Charles I's execution, Banqueting House is definitely worth a visit.

Each year, on 30th January a service in Banqueting House remembers the execution of King Charles I.

Please note that Banqueting House regularly closes early as it is also used as events venue. Consult the website for confirmation.

The Battle of Britain London Monument

Unveiled in 2005, this memorial includes incredibly lifelike bronze depictions of the airmen in the 1940 Battle of Britain. The way that movement has been captured is simply incredible.

The monument also contains plaques remembering the 3000 airmen and allies who fought in the battle.

It is less than a minute's walk to the Royal Air Force Memorial located further up the Victoria Embankment.

 Westminster   Victoria Embankment, WC2N 5. Near Westminster pier.   24/7 - Public area

Westminster Cathedral

 Victoria

 Gallery: Ad: £6, Conc: £3. Exhibition: Ad: £5, Conc: £2.50.

 Tower & Exhibition: Mon to Fri 9:30 to 17:00, closes 1 hour later on Sat and Sun.

 westminster cathedral.org.uk

 42 Francis Street, SW1P 1QW

Westminster Cathedral is often missed by visitors to the city, despite many stopping at the more famous Westminster Abbey. The two churches are not to be confused.

Even during peak summer season, this church is often very empty as far as visitors are concerned and admission into the church is free.

Westminster Cathedral is the principal Roman Catholic church in the UK and dates from 1903 (whereas Westminster Abbey is Protestant).

Many people walk past the church and miss it, maybe even assuming it is a mosque due to the large tower and unusual architecture.

The tower is actually home to a viewing gallery (with lift access), and the church houses an exhibition – Treasures of Westminster Cathedral – where you can see rare collections of objects and learn about the church's construction.

Both of these activities are paid admission. However, entry into the church to see the beautiful mosaics and marble-work (or for prayer) is free at all times.

Eat

The Northall (Corinthia Hotel)
Tube: *Embankment*
Website: *bit.ly/northall*
Phone: *0207 930 8181*
Address: *Corinthia Hotel, WC2N 5AE*
Hours: *Breakfast: 6:30 to 10:30 on weekdays, 7:00 to 11:00 on weekends. Lunch: Mon to Sat 12:00 to 15:00, Sun 12:30 to 16:00. Dinner: Daily 17:30 to 23:00.*

Delicious British-inspired food with incredible presentation, excellent service and an amazing setting. A La Carte breakfast is served or a buffet at £34 per adult. The Express Lunch set menu is £25 for 2 courses, or £29 for 3. A Theatre set menu is similarly priced. Also serves a Sunday brunch. A la Carte mains are £14 to £35.

Gustoso
Tube: *Victoria*
Website: *ristorantegustoso. co.uk*

Phone: *0207 834 5778*
Address: *35 Willow Place, SW1P 1JH*
Hours: *Mon to Thur 12:00 to 22:30, Fri & Sat 12:00 to 23:00, Sun 12:30 to 21:30.*

Delicious food with good service. Prices are fair with pasta mains from £9 to £14, and meat or fish-based main courses at £10 to £17.50. Specials are also available for a rotating set of dishes each and every day. Reservations are accepted and highly recommended.

Brutti & Boni
Tube: *Gloucester Road and High Street Kensington*
Website: *bruttiandboni.com*
Phone: *0207 589 2260*
Address: *14 Gloucester Road, SW7 4RB*
Hours: Closed Mon. Tues to Fri 8:00 to 18:00. Sat 9:00 to 18:00 & Sun 10:00 to 18:00.

More of a café than a restaurant with tasty and authentic Italian food

with only 4 tables inside. It is the perfect place for a lunchtime snack, or something a little bit filling. Pasta dishes are £7 to £8, delicious tortellini is £10, with focaccia and pizza slices at £4 to £6. Great prices and great quality.

The Lord Moon of the Mall
Tube: *Charing Cross*
Website: *bit.ly/moonmall*
Phone: *0207 839 7701*
Address: *16 Whitehall, SW1A 2DY*
Hours: *Sun 8:00 to 23:00, Mon to Thur 8:00 to 23:30, Fri & Sat 8:00 to midnight.*

A great spot for British pub classics in central London. This is a chain pub with decent food for the price in a prime location. This is a popular establishment and finding a table can be hard. Breakfast is £2.30 to £5 including a drink - traditional English breakfast is an option. Classic pub meals are £6.50 to £12.

Stay

Hotel 41
Tube: *Victoria*
Website: *41hotel.com*
Phone: *0207 300 0041*
Address: *41 Buckingham Palace Road, SW1W 0PS*

This boutique hotel is just steps from Buckingham Palace, with only 30 rooms and suites. Each room is unique. Service is exemplary with two members of staff for every guest and a 24-hour butler.

Rooms start at £295 per night, and suites at £599. TripAdvisor rates this as the

number 1 hotel in London.

Corinthia Hotel
Tube: *Embankment*
Website: *corinthia.com/ hotels/london*
Phone: *0207 930 8181*
Address: *Whitehall Place, SW1A 2BD*

This hotel's location, modern interiors and restaurants make this one of the best places to stay in London Service is exceptional, and the fitness suite and indoor pool are particularly impressive. Rooms from £357 per night.

The Grosvenor Hotel
Tube: *Victoria*
Website: *bit.ly/grosvictoria*
Phone: *0871 376 9038*
Address: *101 Buckingham Palace Road, SW1W 0SJ*

Next to Victoria station, and a 5-minute stroll from Buckingham Palace, this 4-star hotel offers reasonable prices, especially considering the location.

This hotel is right next to busy Victoria Station so some noise should be expected. Rooms from £120.

The Southbank

The Southbank area that we are describing here is a small strip of land on the south side of the river Thames, opposite Westminster and Embankment.

This is a very popular area with visitors, especially since the year 2000 when the London Eye opened.

We have also included The Imperial War Museum in this area, although it is a 10 to 15-minute walk away.

The London Eye, London Dungeon, London Aquarium, Shrek's Adventure and Madame Tussauds are all attractions operated by Merlin Entertainments. All of these, except Madame Tussauds, are located in the same building on the South Bank.

Visit the ticket desk at any of these, or online, and consider the multi-attraction tickets on sale. These can offer big savings.

See and Do

London Aquarium

 Waterloo

 Ad: £26, Age 3 to 15: £21, Family: £88

 Weekdays 10:00 to 18:00. Weekends 9:30 to 19:00

 visitsealife.com/london

 County Hall, Westminster Bridge Road, SE1 7PB

This is London's largest aquarium. Inside you can see sharks, touch rays, marvel at the seahorses, delight at the penguins and much more. Learn about fish from around the world, and then bring it all back home by learning about the River Thames.

Throughout the day, talks and feeding times allow you to get to know these animals a bit better. You can see feeding sessions throughout the day for the octopuses, rays, penguins, sharks, seahorses and more.

There are also several VIP experiences available at an extra charge, including: a behind the scenes tour, turtle feeding, shark feeding, snorkelling with sharks, and a marine biologist experience.

A typical visit of the attraction will take about 2 hours, plus any time you take to attend optional talks and feedings.

London Eye

 Waterloo

 Ad: £26, Age 3 to 15: £21

 Daily 10:00 to 18:00. Late closings up to 23:00 at peak times.

 londoneye.com

 London Eye, Westminster Bridge Road, SE1 7PB

For a unique view of London, step into one of the viewing capsules on the 135-metre tall London Eye. It is the world's tallest cantilevered Ferris wheel and from the top, you can see up to 40km on a clear day.

The London Eye's 32 capsules constantly rotate and a journey onboard takes 30 minutes – it doesn't feel like you are moving as you go around steadily, yet gives you the perfect amount of time to get all the photos you want.

On board you can gaze across London, sit on the seats in the middle of the capsules, or use one of the onboard tablets to learn about the monuments around you.

As a crowd management measure, tickets bought for the London Eye are allocated 30-minute slots. You must visit during this slot to ensure you can ride. Fast Track tickets are also available for those in a rush and flexible time tickets are also available.

We strongly recommend you buy tickets in advance as tickets sell out in busy periods. We would recommend booking just a day or two in advance if you have a specific time slot due to London's changeable weather hampering visibility.

The London Eye experience can also be personalised to something even more special with the option of a private capsule; a champagne experience is also available, and there are many other options.

Originally, the London Eye was known as the Millennium Wheel and was only intended to be in place for the year 2000. It is now one of the most popular attractions in the UK.

Note: Every year in January, the London Eye shuts for its annual maintenance, usually during the second and third weeks of the month. The London Eye also closes early on December 31st as London's fireworks display is held on the London Eye itself.

London Dungeon

Waterloo

£ Ad: £30, Age 4 to 15: £24

Term time: 10:00 to 17:00 Mon-Wed & Fri; 11:00 to 17:00 Thurs, and 10:00 to 18:00 weekends. Longer in school holidays.

thedungeons. com/london/en/

County Hall, Westminster Bridge Rd, SE1 7PB

The London Dungeon has been a staple of the city since 1974, and moved to County Hall in 2012.

With its relocation, came the addition of new scenes, the change of others. Throughout the adventure you will take a boat ride for traitors, 'drop in' on some hangings, experience Sweeney Todd's barber shop, learn about Guy Fawkes, feel what its like to visit a Plague Doctor, encounter Jack the Ripper, and much more.

A Victorian Tavern at the end allows you to enjoy a complimentary drink too!

Inside, guests are put into groups of about 20 people and are taken from scene to scene. Each scene depicts a period or event from London's gruesome past and uses actors and audience interaction to bring it to life. As well as the scenes with actors, there are also a couple of rides interspersed during the experience. Special physical effects throughout the experience add to the fun.

The full experience lasts approximately 110 minutes and is not recommended for the squeamish – it is not a 'jump out' horror-maze type attraction, and you will

learn quite a bit, but wimps should beware as there are some scares. Teenagers and young adults in particular are often the biggest fans of this attraction.

This attraction operates on a time-slot ticketed system, if tickets are pre-booked. On the door tickets are more expensive and will require you to enter a queue, which can be an hour or longer during peak times. Fast track and VIP tickets are also available.

The Dungeon also occasionally offers Lates - adult-only after-hour experiences.

Shrek's Adventure

 Waterloo

 Ad (16+): £27.50, Children: £22

 shreksadventure.com

 County Hall, Westminster Bridge Road, SE1 7PB

 Sun to Fri 10:00 to 17:00, and Sat 10:00 to 18:00

Shrek's Adventure provides some child-minded fun in the heart of the city. The attraction is targeted at kids aged 6 to 12 and takes you on a journey through Shrek's swamp.

The entire experience lasts about 75 minutes and uses a similar format to the London Dungeon whereby guests are put into groups of about 20 and go from scene to scene immersed in Shrek's world.

Along the way, guests can expect to meet Shrek and his friends, go on a crazy 4D bus ride, get lost in a mirror maze and much more in this interactive experience. Kids even get to take part in some scenes.

Tickets to this attraction are timed and it is possible that they sell out during busier periods of the year.

Imperial War Museum

 Lambeth North or Elephant & Castle

 Free

 iwm.org.uk

 Daily 10:00 to 18:00

 Imperial War Museum, Lambeth Road, SE1 6HZ

The Imperial War Museum is a fascinating collection of artefacts focusing on WWII. The museum is made up of several permanent collections, including the build up, the war, post-war life, and more.

There is also a permanent collection featuring families during WWII, the story of the First World War, a very haunting Holocaust Exhibition, and a 'Curiosities of War' section, which contains some unusual objects.

This museum is absolutely worth exploring, and regularly holds free temporary exhibitions and should be high up your list. It is truly a world-class experience.

Eat

Locale - County Hall
Tube: *Waterloo*
Website: *localerestaurants. com/southbank.php*
Phone: 0207 401 6734
Address: *County Hall, 3b Belvedere Road, SE1 7EP*
Hours: *Sun to Thur 12:00 to 22:30, closes at 23:00 on Fri & Sat.*

Locale's food is tasty, plentiful and the service is good too. Pasta and Risotta is £9 to £14, with meat and fish dishes at £15 to £23, pizzas are around £10, and salads are £8 to £10. There is also a bar.

Skylon
Tube: *Waterloo and Embankment*
Website: *skylon-restaurant. co.uk*
Phone: *0207 654 7800*
Address: *Southbank Centre, Belvedere Road, Royal Festival Hall, SE1 8XX*
Hours: Lunch: *Mon to Sat 12:00 to 14:30, Sun 12:00 to*

15:30. Dinner: *Mon to Sat 17:30 to 22:30. On Sunday only grill and bar are open.*

For a view of the River Thames and delicious food, Skylon may just be the best place on the Southbank. Staff are attentive and the location includes a bar and grill. A la Carte mains are £24 to £39. A 6-course tasting menu is £59. The set menu is £25 for 2 courses, and £30 for 3. Reservations are recommended.

Brasserie Joel
Tube: *Waterloo*
Website: *brasseriejoel.co.uk*
Phone: *0207 620 7272*
Address: *First Floor, Park Plaza Westminster Bridge Hotel, SE1 7UT*
Hours: Lunch: *Mon to Fri 12:00 to 14:00. No lunch on Sat. Sun 12:30 to 15:30. Dinner: Mon to Sat 17:30 to 22:30. Sun 17:30 to 21:30.*

Brasserie Joel serves

authentic French dishes, and has won numerous awards. The setting, presentation and service area all excellent. Mains are £14.50 to £32.50. Set menus at lunch are £14 for 2 courses and £16 for 3 courses, and at dinner £17 and £20 respectively. Reservations are recommended.

Troia
Tube: *Waterloo*
Website: *troia-restaurant. co.uk*
Phone: *0207 633 9309*
Address: *3f Belvedere Road, County Hall, SE1 7GQ*
Hours: *Mon to Sat 12:00 to 23:30, Sun 12:00 to 22:30*

For great quality Turkish try Troia. This place is more of a café/bistro than a posh dining location, meaning it is a more relaxed atmosphere. Mains are £10 to £15 with grilled Turkish items, as well as staples such as steaks, pasta, salads and seafood.

Stay

Park Plaza Westminster Bridge
Tube: *Waterloo and Westminster*
Website: *bit.ly/plazawest*
Phone: *0844 415 6790*
Address: *200 Westminster Bridge Road, SE1 7UT*

This 4-star hotel is in a fantastic location. A five-minute stroll takes you to Big Ben, the London Eye, London Dungeon and other attractions. Westminster Abbey is 10 minutes away. We like the modern interiors of the rooms and the dining selection. Rooms from £161.

Premier Inn London County Hall
Tube: *Waterloo and Westminster*
Website: *bit.ly/countypremi*
Phone: *0871 527 8648*
Address: *Belvedere Road, Westminster, SE1 7PB*

Premier Inn provides good value for money, in good locations and decent rooms. This 3-star hotel is no exception. Round the corner is the London Eye and Big Ben. The location is fantastic; rooms are basic but of good quality. For a well-priced base, this is a good bet. Rooms from £79.

London Marriott Hotel County Hall
Tube: *Waterloo and Westminster*
Website: *bit.ly/marcount*
Phone: *020 7928 5200*
Address: *Belvedere Road, Westminster, SE1 7PB*

This 5-Star Marriott offers rooms with views of the London Eye or Big Ben, and the location is perfect. Amenities include a pool and a fitness centre, and rooms are air conditioned. There's a steakhouse and bar, a lounge with afternoon tea, and a terrace. Rooms from £242.

West End & Trafalgar Square

The West End is the heart of London's nightlife scene, with bars, clubs and pubs abound in this area. Soho, in particular, is the bohemian district of London.

The West End is home to over 55 theatres (more that anywhere else in the world) and provides a huge array of dining experiences. Leicester Square in the heart of the area is home to red-carpet film premieres. Chinatown is also in this area.

Mayfair is also located nearby, the home of multi-millionaires and billionaires, with house prices regularly topping £40 million. Take a stroll through Mayfair and see the beautiful buildings, with luxury shopping in New Bond Street and Old Bond Street, the beautiful area of Shepherd's Market, and Mount Street with luxury boutiques. More affordable high-street style shopping can be found on Regent Street and Oxford Street.

For cultural delights, head to Trafalgar Square and take in the National Gallery and National Portrait Gallery – both of which are free.

There is a good chance you will be spending quite a while in this area of London with its multitude of things to do.

See and Do

Royal Academy of Arts

 Green Park and Piccadilly

 Varies by exhibition.

 royalacademy.org.uk

 Burlington House, Piccadilly, London, W1J 0BD

 Sat to Thurs 10:00 to 18:00, with a late closing on Fri at 22:00. Last admission: 30 minutes before closing.

The Royal Academy of Arts holds a unique position in that it does not really house a permanent collection, and has constantly changing exhibitions. These exhibitions are all paid entry but the Royal Academy prides itself on providing some of the most interesting and rare exhibitions anywhere in the world, so the cost of admission is usual well worth it.

Talks are also regularly held at the Royal Academy and the vast majority of these are free; there are often other special events too.

The Royal Academy also regularly runs one-hour tours covering the art, architecture and history of the building. Check the website for the exact timings of the tours – the tours are free, but donations are welcome.

Chinatown

 Piccadilly Circus & Leicester Square

 Free

 24/7 - Public area

 Gerrard St, W1D 6JS

Every major city has a Chinatown and London's is located right by the hustle and bustle of Piccadilly Circus.

As soon as you enter Chinatown, you are likely to encounter one of two situations depending on the time of day: either a very peaceful space, or a bustling atmosphere.

As far as food is concerned, there is something for everyone and for every price range. Many places here are cash only so be sure to ask before getting a table at a restaurant, or in loading up on purchases in shops.

This is a small Chinatown unlike some other cities and, we wouldn't go out of our way to go here deliberately unless you fancy a bit of Chinese food.

Piccadilly Circus

 Piccadilly Circus

 Free

 24/7 - Public area

 Piccadilly Circus, W1D 7ET

Piccadilly Circus anchors one side of the West End with the famous Piccadilly Lights, the giant advertising billboards.

The first sign was put up back in 1908, and it was the world's first set of outdoor electric lights. They have been upgraded over the years and are now only on one corner of the area.

You can regularly see street performers in this area. From dancers to beatboxers and mimes to singers.

Piccadilly Circus is well known for the angel-like Statue of Anteros, atop the Shaftesbury Memorial Fountain. This is dedicated to the 7th Earl of Shaftesbury who famously fought to stop children becoming chimney sweeps. Anteros is The Angel of Christian Charity, but he is often mistaken for his brother Eros – the Greek god of love.

The Criterion Theatre is also located in this area – Theatreland's only underground performance space; Lillywhites next door is known as a premium sports retailer with attractive prices.

Notable roads off Piccadilly Circus include Piccadilly, Regent Street and Haymarket for access to Pall Mall and Trafalgar Square. Most of these are filled with shops.

National Gallery

 Charing Cross and Leicester Square

 Free

 10:00 to 18:00 (daily) and 10:00 to 21:00 (Fri)

 nationalgallery.org.uk

 The National Gallery, Trafalgar Square, WC2N 5DN

The National Gallery is one of our favourite museums in London and it is free admission to all.

It houses some priceless works of art including notably Van Gogh's "Sunflowers", Monet's "Water Lilies" and Seurat's "Bathers at Asnières" amongst many others.

The paintings on offer cover several centuries and the building's interior architecture is worth visiting for alone.

The paid-for audio guides are thoroughly recommended at £4 per adult and £3.50 for concessions. Several different audio tours are available. The National Gallery website also has suggested walking tours that you can print out or follow along with you on a smartphone or tablet.

The National Gallery also has a paid-for 'Sainsbury Wing', which features temporary exhibitions and collections.

The gallery is closed on 1st January and 24th to 26th December.

National Portrait Gallery

Charing Cross and Leicester Square

Free

10:00 to 18:00 (daily) and 10:00 to 21:00 (Fri)

npg.org.uk

St. Martin's Place, WC2H 0H

Located just off Trafalgar Square is a collection of over 200,000 portraits where you can explore royalty, see contemporary paintings and even photographs of famous faces. The museum is certainly worth a visit if you are in the area..

Trafalgar Square

 Charing Cross and Leicester Square

 Free

 24/7 - Public area

 Trafalgar Square, WC2N 5DN

Trafalgar Square celebrates Lord Admiral Horatio Nelson's victory in 1805 against the French and Spanish forces at Cape Trafalgar. Nelson's Column dominates the square, at 135 feet tall it is the same height as his ship (HMS Victory). Atop of the column is an 18-foot statue of Nelson.

The square is recognised by visitors from across the globe, and it was even used as inspiration in George Orwell's 1984 where it is referred to as Victory Square.

The famous fountains on the square date from the 1930s and were designed by Sir Edwin Lutyens. The lions around the base of Nelson's column date from the 1860s by Edwin Landseer.

Statues adorn the corners of the square: George IV (also known as the Prince Regent), Sir Charles James Napier (the British Commander-in-Chief in India in the 1840s), and Sir Henry Havelock (a British general). The fourth plinth remained empty until 1999. Since 2005, a different sculpture has been placed on the plinth every year or two.

As of late 2017, the statue is "Really Good" by David Shrigley, a giant thumbs-up with the thumb rising to 10 metres in height. In 2018, a new sculpture will arrive called "The Invisible Enemy Should Not Exist", a recreation of a sculpture destroyed by Islamic State in 2015 - the sculpture is *Lamassu*, a winged bull and protective god. The sculpture will be made of syrup cans from Iraq.

Buildings here include:
• The Canadian, South African, and Ugandan High Commissions
• St. Martin in the Fields Church, located to the right of The National Gallery is the church where royal births are registered. It is famous for its Crypt Café with warm food at pub prices in a beautiful underground setting.
• The National Gallery and The National Portrait Gallery, which are covered on the previous page.

Leicester Square

 Leicester Square

 Leicester Square, W1D 6AP

 24/7 - Public area

Leicester Square is in many ways the heart of the West End. It is where film premieres take place for major films, including James Bond, Harry Potter and Star Wars. The square is home to numerous places to eat and you can enjoy the multitude of souvenir shops available here too.

Theatre fans should stop by TKTS – The Official London Theatre Ticket Booth. It sells same-day half price and discounted theatre tickets for many London shows, as well as full-priced tickets for other shows. You can check online in advance for what tickets they have on sale that day, and the next couple of days. The booth is open from 10:00 to 19:00 Monday to Saturday, and 11:00 to 16:30 on Sunday.

Covent Garden

 Covent Garden

 24/7 - Public area

 coventgarden
.london

 Covent Garden
Piazza, WC2E 7BB

Once the place where Westminster Abbey had its convent garden, this location is now a beautiful pedestrianised square surrounded by street performers, cafés, restaurants, markets, shops and the London Transport Museum.

Make sure to explore the covered area in the middle of the square and use the steps to go into the underground portion where there are beautiful, quaint little shops to explore.

There is more on Covent Garden later in the shopping section of this guide.

London Transport Museum

 Covent Garden

 Ad: £17.50, Under 18: Free, Conc: £15.

 Daily 10:00 to 18:00

 ltmuseum.co.uk

 Covent Garden
Piazza, WC2E 7BB

The London Transport Museum is situated in the heart of Covent Garden. It explains and conserves the heritage of London's transportation, telling its story spanning 200 years.

You can learn about how London's basic transport system functioned in the past, the arrival of the world's first underground railway, and how transport is intricately linked with London's transformation and expansion.

This is one of our favourite museums in London and it is truly fascinating seeing how important transportation has been to London's evolution.

The London Transport Museum offers many interactive exhibitions, as well as actual buses and underground trains dating back over 100 years.

Individual tickets purchased for the museum are valid for unlimited visits for the named person during one year.

Cleopatra's Needle

Cleopatra's Needle is the oldest outdoor monument in London – it is between 3000 and 3500 years old. The Needle is situated on the Victoria Embankment, a short stroll from Embankment station.

Cleopatra's Needle is an ancient Egyptian obelisk presented to the UK by Egyptian ruler Muhammad Ali to commemorate the

Embankment	Free
24/7	Victoria Embankment, London, WC2N 6

victory at the Battle of the Nile in 1819. The Needle has two "twins" in Paris and New York City.

Fun Fact: Curiously, the

sphinxes at the base of the obelisk were placed incorrectly and instead of looking outwards to "guard" the needle, they are just staring at it instead.

Handel House Museum & Jimi Hendrix Flat

 Bond Street and Oxford Circus

 Ad: £10 for admission to both the museum and the flat. Child: £5

 handelhendrix.org

 25 Brook Street, Mayfair, W1K 4HB

 Mon to Sat 11:00 to 18:00. Closed Sundays.

These two locations are right next door to each other on Brook Street. Number 25 was previously home to Handel who lived and composed there for 36 years to 1759, and the top

floor of the house next door was Jimi Hendrix's flat in 1968 and 1969.

At the Handel House Museum, you can see four restored rooms, as well as

temporary exhibitions about the man himself. The main living area of Hendrix's flat has also been restored, and an exhibition about Hendrix is also in place.

London Film Museum

 Covent Garden

 Ad: £14.50, Ages 5 to 15 and Conc: £9.50, Family: £38

 londonfilm museum.com

 45 Wellington Street, Covent Garden, WC2E 7BN

 10:00 to 18:00 from Sun to Fri, and 10:00 to 19:00 on Sat

This film museum houses temporary exhibitions.

After the success of a Star Wars exhibit, Bond in Motion is now at the museum – this is the largest official collection of original Bond vehicles ever in London with over 100 original vehicles and artefacts spanning all 24 films.

From the vehicles themselves to concept art, and the unique inventions that make Bond the man he is, there is much to see. There is no set end date for this exhibition at the time of writing.

Somerset House & The Courtauld Gallery

 Temple and Covent Garden

 Embankment - Varies. Courtauld - Ad: £8, Conc: £7, Under 18: Free

 Galleries 10:00 to 18:00 daily, Other areas 07:30 or 08:00 to 23:00

 somersethouse .org.uk and courtauld.ac.uk

 Somerset House, Strand, WC2R 1LA

Somerset House is a cultural centre hosting several artistic events. The centre courtyard of the building is home to an ice rink in the winter, and dancing fountains in the summer.

There is also the Embankment Gallery area that contains temporary exhibitions; the Courtauld Gallery is home to French impressionist paintings.

Public areas of the building are free to explore, but the galleries are paid admission.

Free guided tours of the building are offered on select days of the week. Check the website for exact dates and timing.

Benjamin Franklin House

 Charing Cross and Embankment

 Historical Experience: Ad: £8, Conc: £6, Under 16: Free. Architectural Tours: Ad: £6 Under 16: Free.

 benjaminfranklin house.org

 36 Craven Street, WC2N 5NF

 Set show and tour times from 12:00 to 16:15 Wed to Mon. Box office opens at 10:30. Closed to the public on Tues.

Visit the only surviving home of where the US Founding Father, Benjamin Franklin, spent sixteen years living and working on the eve of the American Revolution.

The house dates from the 1730s and still has many of the original features, including a staircase and windows.

There are 25-minute architectural tours of the location, as well as a 45-minute "historical experience", which combines learning with theatre.

Royal Courts of Justice

 Temple and Holborn

 0207 947 6000 (07789 751248 for tours)

 justice.gov.uk/ courts/rcj-rolls-building

 Strand, WC2A 2LL

Dating from 1882, this stunning building is home to the High Court and Court of Appeal of England and Wales.

Members of the public can go inside and sit in the public gallery to hear court in session, apart from certain private matters. There is no charge to do this. The building is open to the public daily weekdays between 9:30am and 4:30pm - photography is not allowed inside the building.

In addition, the RCJ runs very under-publicised tours of the building delving into its architecture, art and the history of the building. Tours run for about two hours and are priced at £13 per adult, £10 per child (under 15). These tours run regularly, subject to there being enough interest.

Eat

The West End area of London has a fantastic variety of culinary delights from Italian to Chinese, Japanese to British, and American to Indian.

This area is filled with both Londoners and visitors to the city, meaning that there are many places that are 'tourist traps' with high prices and sub-par food, so check restaurant reviews before choosing where to eat.

Having said that, the West End does contain some of the best places to eat in the whole city, so it is well worth making a stop here.

There are buffets, Table Service and fast food places in every direction you look, and prices on the whole are competitive as restaurants want to attract theatre-goers and evening crowds.

Hawksmoor – Air Street
Tube: *Piccadilly Circus*
Website: *thehawksmoor. com/locations/airstreet/*
Phone: *0207 406 3980*
Address: *5a Air Street, W1J 0AD*
Hours: *Lunch: Mon to Fri 12:00 to 15:00. Dinner: Mon to Thurs 17:00 to 22:30, & Fri 17:00 to 23:00. Sat 12:00 to 23:00. Sun 12:00 to 22:30.*

This upscale Seafood and Steak restaurant has become very popular over the last few years. They serve some of the best cuts of steak we have ever eaten. Perhaps surprisingly for a steak place, the seafood here is delicious too.

Prices are on the higher end as this is a premium experience. Seafood is priced at £20 to £48 for a whole fish, with Turbot priced at £13 per 100g, and the delicious Dartmouth Lobster at £5 per 100g. Steaks are £18.50 to £35, and vary in size from 300g to 400g. Large cuts are £8.25 to £13 per 100g, starting at 500g in size.

A Sunday roast option is £20. The express menu is a particularly good deal at £25 for two courses, and £28 for three. It is available Monday to Saturday until 6:30pm.

This location is just seconds from Piccadilly Circus. Other Hawksmoor London locations include: Seven Dials (Covent Garden), Guildhall and Spitalfields (in The City), and Knightsbridge. Reservations are recommended.

Quattro Passi (QP LDN)
Tube: *Green Park*
Phone: *0203 096 1444*
Address: *34 Dover Street, W1S 4NG*
Hours: *Daily 12:00 to 15:00, and 18:30 to 22:30 (last orders). Closed Sun.*

This upscale Italian restaurant boasts lavish interiors, a signature menu and a Michelin-Starred Head Chef, Antonio Mellino. Appetizers/antipasti are £12 to £20. Pasta dishes are £16 to £22, and other mains such as fish and meat are £25 to £35. A "business lunch" offer is available Monday to Friday from 12:00 to 15:00, with 2 courses priced at £26, and 3 courses at £34.

Prices are on the higher side but we feel the experience, service and taste merit this. Reservations are recommended.

Misato
Tube: *Piccadilly Circus & Leicester Square*
Phone: *0207 734 0808*
Address: *11 Wardour Street, W1D 6PG*
Hours: *Daily 12:00 to 23:00*

Japanese food just steps away from Chinatown? That's right! Misato is one of the most affordable quality meals in central London. 8-piece mixed sashimi sets are £7.50, sushi pieces are £1 each, and maki costs even less; you can have a decent meal here for less than £15 per person. Bento boxes are £8.50, and they also serve light meals and rice dishes at £5 to £8 each. Even the beers are under £3.

With good quality food, and large portions, at an affordable price, Misato is great spot to dine at. There may be waits to get in at peak periods as this is a popular place and is quite small. Misato does not currently have its own website, and does not accept reservations.

Yauatcha
Tube: *Piccadilly Circus & Leicester Square*
Website: *yauatcha.com*
Phone: *0207 494 8888*
Address: *15-17 Broadwick*

Street, W1F 0DL
Hours: Daily 12:00 to 22:00, with a late closing at 22:30 on Fri and Sat.

Serving some of the best contemporary Cantonese food in London, Yauatcha offers upscale dining.

A la Carte prices vary wildly, from the £9.20 egg fried rice to the £38 Lobster vermicelli pot. Lunch and dinner "signature" menus are also available for £40 and £45 per person, with a minimum of two people dining.

The service is attentive and the interior is simple but elegant. The cake selection is to die for. Reservations are recommended.

Savoir Faire

Tube: *Tottenham Court Road & Holborn*
Website: *savoir.co.uk*
Phone: *0207 436 0707*
Address: *42 New Oxford Street, WC1A 1EP*
Hours: *Daily 12:00 to 22:30*

With London's French population standing at over 66,000 and counting, it's no surprise to find quality French fare in the city. Savoir Faire is located on the edge of the West End, less than a 2-minute walk from The British Museum.

At Savoir Faire everything is prepared fresh on the premises – from the mains, to the bread, the sauces and even the dessert.

A two-course set lunch menu is just £14.90. The a la carte lunch menu includes salads, burgers, omelets and sandwiches – all priced at £5 to £10. Muscles, beef and lamb are £7 to £18.

A 2-course dinner menu is £23.90, with a vegetarian menu at £14.90. Main courses such as Rib Eye Steak, Fillet of Sea Bass and Duck Margaret are all £18 a la Carte at dinner.

All meals include a basket of fresh bread, as is customary in France, and in our opinion, the food is very affordably priced and of excellent quality. Reservations are accepted.

Stay

The Ritz

Tube: *Tottenham Court Road & Holborn*
Website: *theritzlondon.com*
Phone: *0207 836 4343*
Address: *150 Piccadilly, W1J 9BR*

Founded by César Ritz in 1906, this 5-star hotel was intended to be the best in London, and in many ways it is. The interiors are beautiful and its easy to understand why The Royal Family has held several events here.

There are 111 rooms and 23 suites at The Ritz, so it always retains an exclusive feel. The smallest rooms are only 215 ft^2 (20 m^2) in size, however.

With the casino in the basement, and the afternoon tea service, there is always something to do. The service is unrivalled.

Rooms at The Ritz start at £396 per night.

The Savoy

Tube: *Charing Cross and Embankment*
Website: *fairmont.com/savoy-london*
Phone: *0207 836 4343*
Address: *Strand, WC2R 0EU*

This 5-star hotel is another well-known hotel in central London, and it is very well located. Within a radius of a 15-minute walk you can reach the London Eye, Big Ben, Trafalgar Square, and the West End. Some rooms offer great river views.

The hotel was the first to be lit by electric lamps, have electric lifts, and en-suite bathrooms in each room. Things we now take for granted!

The hotel has 4 restaurants, 2 bars, a spa and pool, and a health club. Rooms start at £351 per night.

Travelodge London Covent Garden

Tube: *Covent Garden and Temple*
Website: *travelodge.co.uk*
Phone: *0871 984 6245*
Address: *10 Drury Lane, High Holborn, WC2B 5RE*

Travelodge is a budget hotel chain with simple, clean rooms. Set in the heart of the West End, a short walk in any direction will take you to a number of attractions.

Amenities are basic with no on-site restaurant. There are several Travelodge hotels in central London.

Rooms at this 2-star hotel start at just £49 per night.

Kensington & The Museums

Kensington is one of the most affluent areas in the world, with house prices in the millions; a 5-bedroom luxury flat was even recently sold for £140 million.

The area is very much residential but also offers a collection of London's finest museums. Those looking for a bit of royalty will be pleased to find both Kensington Palace in a park called Kensington Gardens, and the Royal Albert Hall, a live performance venue.

Shoppers will not be disappointed with the selection of luxury goods on offer on High Street Kensington, King's Road, and Harrods – the largest department store in Europe at over 1 million square feet in size.

Finally, sports fans can visit Stamford Bridge, Chelsea F.C.'s stadium.

See and Do

Natural History Museum

South Kensington

£ Free

Daily 10:00 to 17:50.

nhm.ac.uk

Cromwell Rd, SW7 5BD

The Natural History Museum has long been a popular haunt for both Londoners and tourists alike but since most museums were made free in 2001, its popularity has soared.

The museum was purpose-built and opened in 1881 moving much of the collection from the British Museum here.

There are a wide variety of permanent exhibitions. Throughout your visit you can marvel at dinosaur skeletons and an animatronic T-Rex, see geological finds, explore the enormous Mammals area, and even walk past scientists working at the museum's Darwin Centre.

The museum also offers fascinating temporary exhibitions, which are paid admission, as well as special events such as a 'Night at the Museum'-style sleepover.

Science Museum

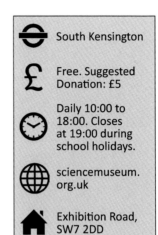

South Kensington

£ Free. Suggested Donation: £5

Daily 10:00 to 18:00. Closes at 19:00 during school holidays.

sciencemuseum.org.uk

Exhibition Road, SW7 2DD

Located right next to the Natural History Museum, the Science Museum is absolutely fascinating and one of our favourite museums.

Inside you can learn all about outer space and the moon landings, take part in interactive exhibitions, see how steam trains and airplanes have revolutionised transport and much more.

An excellent paid admission area, called Wonderlab, is dedicated to young children with shows and interactive exhibitions making learning fun. Tickets to this area are £10 for adults and £8 per child. Discounts are available for families.

Also inside the museum is an IMAX screen showing scientific movies, as well as a simulator attraction and numerous kids play areas. There are also many places to shop and eat. Temporary exhibitions and special events mean there are always a multitude of reasons to keep coming back.

On the last Wednesday of each month, from 18:45 to 22:00, the museum hosts 'Lates', a free adult-only night.

The "free" aspect of this museum has changed. They now require you to go past a ticket desk where staff will ask you if you wish to donate to enter. It is not compulsory but it can be awkward. The suggested £5 donation is exceptional value but we'd rather they charge properly or just make it open access with donation points on the way out like other museums.

Victoria & Albert Museum

 South Kensington

 Free

 Daily 10:00 to 17:45. Late closing at 22:00 on Fri.

 vam.ac.uk

 Cromwell Road, SW7 2RL

An absolute gem of a museum that shouldn't be missed by art lovers.

We like to think of the V&A as London's *Musée du Louvre* in terms of grandeur and variety of exhibitions.

Collections include architecture, books, ceramics, fashion, furniture, painting, textiles and much more. A particularly large collection of items from 1600 to 1850 are also on display.

Many temporary exhibitions are offered throughout the year too – these require an entry fee.

It is not really a location we would take children to as there is not very much to stimulate their senses, but adults of all ages will appreciate the wonder of the V&A.

The building, courtyard and exhibitions are delightful and we highly recommend a visit.

Saatchi Gallery

 Sloane Square

 Free

 Daily 10:00 to 18:00.

 saatchigallery.com

 Duke of York's HQ, King's Road, SW3 4RY

The Saatchi Gallery is home to contemporary art and has a regularly rotating set of exhibitions.

Curiously, a lot of the art on display here is by lesser-known, or unknown, artists who are subsequently offered the opportunity for shows worldwide – in this way, the gallery is a gem that gives back to artists as much as it inspires visitors.

Most exhibitions are free.

Kensington Palace

 High Street Kensington

 Ad: £16.50, Conc: £13.70, Under 16s: Free

 Daily 10:00 to 17:00 (winter). Extended hours in summer.

 hrp.org.uk/ kensington-palace/

 Kensington Gardens, W8 4PX

The story of Kensington Palace spans back over 400 years to 1605 when the first house was built on this site: a small two-floor building. By 1689, William III and Mary II had bought the house to convert it into a palace.

The palace was the former home of Princess Diana, and is now home to the Duke and Duchess of Cambridge (Prince William and Kate Middleton).

Kensington Palace, unlike many other royal palaces, is open to the public year-round (except 24th to 26th December).

During a visit to the palace you can enjoy the King's Staircase, the King and Queen's state apartments, the "Victoria Revealed" exhibition, and much more.

Brompton Oratory

 South Kensington

 Free

 Daily 06:30 to 20:00

 bromptonoratory. co.uk

 Brompton Road, SW7 2RP

Also known as The Church of the Immaculate Heart of Mary, this astounding Catholic Church dates from 1884 and is worth popping your head in for a few minutes to see.

It is very similar in style to classic Italian basilicas. From the stunning High Altar to St. Wilfred's Chapel, and the beautiful dome to the pulpit, there is a gem around every corner inside.

This is a real working church, and it is not at all a major visitor attraction, so do bear that in mind when visiting. Feel free to attend a service if you are so inclined.

The church is located a few doors down from the Victoria & Albert Museum.

Royal Albert Hall Tours

 South Kensington & Gloucester Road

 Ad: £12.75 to £15.75, Conc: £10.75 to £13.75, Child: £5.75 to £8.75.

 Regular tours: Generally between 10:00 and 15:00.

 royalalberthall.com

 Kensington Gore, SW7 2AP

This 140-year-old location is a music and entertainment venue - we will cover that aspect elsewhere. Tours of this magnificent building are offered:

• **The Grand Tour** is an hour-long journey through the public areas of the Royal Albert Hall, including the beautiful auditorium, the breathtaking view from the Gallery and exclusive access to the Royal Retiring Room. An optional afternoon tea experience can be added for an additional £16.

• **The Secret History Tour** retells the stories of "ghost hunters to gangsters, swindlers and charlatans", and much more.

• **The Behind the Scenes Tour** allows you to visit areas not normally accessible to the public – including under the stage, inside a dressing room, and the loading bay. This tour lasts approximately 1 hour.

• **The Inside Out Architectural Tour** gives you an insight into how this building was designed both inside and out.

During the summer BBC Prom season, a "Story of the Proms" tour is also available.

Brompton Cemetery

 Earl's Court and Fulham Broadway

 Free

 royalparks.org.uk/parks/brompton-cemetery

 Fulham Road, SW10 9UG

 Opens daily at 8:00. Closing times vary seasonally from 16:00 in winter to 20:00 in summer.

Brompton Cemetery is one of Britain's oldest cemeteries, opened in 1840, and has over 205,000 people buried there. It is still a working cemetery to this day and over 700,000 people visit each year.

Notable graves include those of Emmeline Pankhurst (suffragette), William Claude Kirby (first chairman of Chelsea F.C.) and Henry Cole (founded the Victoria & Albert Museum), any others.

Fun Fact: It is said that Beatrix Potter was inspired by some of the names on the tombstones here for her stories – there is even a Peter Rabbett.

Eat

Pizzetta Pizza
Tube: *South Kensington*
Website: *pizzettapizza.com*
Phone: 0207 584 9090
Address: *22 Bute Street,*
South Kensington, SW7 3EX
Hours: *Daily 08:00 to 23:00.*

For fresh pizza in South Kensington, there is no better place than Pizzetta Pizza. This place is small, and informal, and serves some of the best food around.

The pizza is authentic, fresh, and the staff are fantastic. Pizza is sold in £2.50 slices. Pasta dishes are a mere £4.80, and soups are £2.50. The coffee is delicious too, as are the cakes.

For a fantastic deal, visit during Happy Hour on Thursdays from 17:00 to 20:00. They give you a free slice of pizza with every drink. Bargain!

Pizzetta Pizza also has another location in Victoria. No reservations available.

Bosphorus
Tube: *South Kensington*
Phone: *0207 584 4048*
Address: *59 Old Brompton Road, South Kensington, SW7 3JS*
Hours: *Daily 11:00 to 23:30*

Walking past, this may seem like your normal local kebab shop, but that couldn't be further from the truth. The food here is simply delicious, and prices are very affordable. Having been here for 40 years, it is a local staple.

Authentic Turkish kebabs are served in large portions including a pitta and salad, all for £6 to £8.50.

There is a small seating area where you can eat in, or you can get a takeaway.

The Muffin Man Tea Shop
Tube: *Earl's Court and Gloucester Road*
Phone: *0207 937 6652*
Address: *12 Wrights Lane, W8 6TA*
Hours: *Mon to Sat 8:00 to 20:00, Sun 9:00 to 20:00*

For a great breakfast option, make Muffin Man a stop. With a full English breakfast for £9.50, this tea shop provides value for money in the heart of Kensington.

It's not just breakfast, however, as cakes, cupcakes and tea are served all day, as well as salads, sandwiches, paninis and soups. Most items on the menu are £2 to £4, with only a few items over £7.

Stay

The Milestone
Tube: *High Street Kensington*
Website: *milestonehotel.com*
Phone: *0207 917 1000*
Address: *1 Kensington Court, W8 5DL*

This luxury, 5-star hotel's origins date back to 1689. As well as rooms and suites, there are six self-contained apartments. A restaurant, afternoon tea experience, a conservatory area, a spa and a fitness room are some of the on-site amenities. Rooms from £266 per night.

EasyHotel Earl's Court
Tube: *Earl's Court*
Website: *bit.ly/easyearls*
Phone: *0207 373 7457*
Address: *42-48 West Cromwell Road, SW5 9QL*

EasyHotel is our go-to for no-frills stays. From the creators of low-cost airline EasyJet, this is an affordable and clean option. The hotels really are no frills: the cheapest rooms don't even have windows and are tiny; TV and Wi-Fi access are optional extras.

This hotel is close to a tube station and a 15-minute walk to the area's museums. Rooms start at £32 per night.

The Villa Kensington
Tube: *Gloucester Road*
Website: *thevillakensington.co.uk*
Phone: *0207 370 6605*
Address: *10-11 Ashburn Gardens, SW7 4DG*

This 3-star hotel provides affordable accommodation, and is a 10-minute walk from the museums.

A continental breakfast is included in most room rates.

It's an upgrade from EasyHotel in terms of comfort, but this is by not a luxurious place to stay. Rooms from £68 per night.

The City of London

The City of London (or just 'The City') is an area located right in the centre of London itself. Having been founded by the Romans as Londinium about 2000 years ago, The City has morphed into the financial heart of London and the world.

The City has suffered The Great Plague and The Great Fire of London and today is filled with fascinating historical sites in every direction you look, including St. Paul's Cathedral, The Monument and the nearby Tower of London.

Many museums are also dotted around this area.

The City is unusual in that less than 10,000 people live in the area, yet over 500,000 work there in a global financial hub.

See and Do

Inner and Middle Temple

⊖ Temple Temple, EC4Y 7BB

This beautiful area located just by the Victoria Embankment in the City of London is where lawyers and barristers are educated.

Here, you can visit the beautiful grounds, courtyards and gardens, which are a serene oasis in the heart of the city. These usually close at sunset and the area is not accessible on weekends.

Also notable in the area is the stunning Temple Church founded by the Knight's Templar in the late 12th century – this is part of a story that was popularised in The Da Vinci Code.

Fleet Street

Temple and Chancery Lane

Fleet Street, EC4A 2BH

Fleet Street is named after the River Fleet which is a major underground river in London. Up until the 1980s, the street was famous for housing the national newspapers. Fleet Street is still a phrase used today when speaking about newspapers years after they have left the area.

Fleet Street has quite a few notable sights. Starting in the West you can enjoy the Royal Courts of Justice (covered elsewhere in this section). Directly opposite the Courts, pop into Twinings *(address: 216 Strand)* – a tea merchant which has stood here for over 300 years – notice how the shops around this one now tower above it.

You can also see The Temple Bar Memorial monument here which stands proud with a dragon atop – it marks the location of Sir Christopher Wren's previous Temple Bar entrance to the city, which has now been moved next to nearby St. Paul's Cathedral.

Moving further east along Fleet Street, just a few doors down, look for a tiny alleyway called "Hen and Chicken Court", it is here The Demon Barber of Fleet Street – Sweeney Todd – slashed his victims, according to the popular urban legend.

Fleet Street is very well known for its pubs. Our favourite, for atmosphere alone is Ye Olde Cheshire Cheese, which was rebuilt in 1667 – take the staircase downstairs and you will notice how much smaller people were back then: the headroom on the stairs is non-existent. Ye Olde Bank of England does great pies and has a beautiful interior.

St. Bride's Church is another favourite spot of ours and is located just before you reach the end of Fleet Street going east. The unusual spire of this church is said to have been the inspiration for today's multi-tier wedding cake when a local baker used the spire as a template.

By the time you reach the end of Fleet Street you will have a stunning view of nearby St Paul's Cathedral.

Fun Fact: Dragons are the guardians of the City of London, and you will find them on the City of London logo. You will also find dragon statues at most major road entrance to the City of London including Fleet Street, Victoria Embankment, London Bridge and by the Tower of London.

Our favourites – and the grandest – are the Victoria Embankment duo, located just a short stroll from Temple station.

Tower of London

 Tower Hill and Tower Gateway

 Ad: £24.80, Ages 5 to 15: £11.50, Conc: £19.30, Family: £63

 Tues to Sat, 09:00 to 17:30 Mar to Oct, 09:00 to 16:30 Nov to Feb. Opens at 10:00 on Sun and Mon.

 hrp.org.uk/tower-of-london/

 Tower of London, EC3N 4AB

Of all the major visitor attractions in London, the Tower of London is our favourite. It is amazing to see this 900-year-old castle still standing in the very heart of London.

The Tower was originally constructed for William the Conqueror who invaded London in 1066. By 1078, a castle had begun to been built for him on the edge of the City of London. At the time, the Tower of London was just the 'White Tower', that currently stands in the centre of the site. It has expanded immensely over the last 900 years.

The Tower is notorious for having been the home of Henry VIII who had six wives throughout his lifetime.

The sheer size of the Tower of London cannot be underestimated and it is possible to spend an entire day touring this attraction; we recommend a minimum of 3 to 4 hours.

Most of the Tower of London is self-guided, as you choose which areas to explore. However, we recommend you do one of the Yeoman Warder or 'Beefeater' tours to begin your day. These depart from near the entrance to the Tower and are included in the price of admission. The tour lasts approximately one hour, with tours leaving every 30 minutes (last tour 15:30 in summer, 14:30 in winter). Throughout the tour, you will get an inside look at the gruesome history of the Tower and visit some of the key locations throughout the site.

Once you have done the tour, it is time to explore the rest of the site.

Every direction you go in there are intriguing exhibitions to visit, you can also walk across the top of the castle's walls, see The Crown Jewels up close, and much more.

Top Tip: If you have a chance, ask the Warders what its like to live inside the Tower – and yes, they pay rent.

Tower Bridge

 Tower Hill and Tower Gateway

 Exhibition: Ad: £9.80, Ages 5 to 15: £4.20, Conc: £6.80, Family: £22

 Bridge open 24/7. Exhibition: Apr to Sep 10:00 to 17:30, Oct to Mar 09:30 to 17:00. Closed 24th to 26th Dec.

 towerbridge.org.uk

 Tower Bridge Rd, SE1 2UP

There are a few notable bridges on the river Thames that you may wish to explore. Tower Bridge is likely to be at the top of your list, however, as it is undoubtedly the most famous of them all and a true symbol of London.

Unfortunately, despite the bridge's popularity, it is often incorrectly called London Bridge by tourists, which is actually the next bridge down the river.

The bridge itself was unveiled in 1894, and took eight years to build. It was the result of a public competition and Horace Jones (who was an architect) came up with the winning design.

The design allowed foot passengers to cross at all times while allowing ships with large masts through when necessary. The road bridge bascules lift up like a drawbridge, temporarily stopping traffic, to allow the ship to pass. Pedestrians would climb up the towers on either end, walk across the walkway at the top and come back down the other side.

Nowadays, the bridge still lifts up in this same way about 1000 times per year. You can check the Tower Bridge website to see opening times scheduled well into the future.

Today, the lifting process is very quick and pedestrians no longer use the walkways at the top to cross – these are now part of the Tower Bridge Exhibition.

The best place to get photos of the bridge when the bascules are lifted up is from London Bridge which runs parallel, or by the walls of the Tower of London closest to the Thames.

The Tower Bridge Exhibition (paid entry) allows you access inside the towers, as well as the pedestrian walkway across the top and even the engine rooms underneath. 2014 saw the addition of a new glass floor to a small part of each walkway meaning that, if you choose to, you can look straight down at the traffic below.

This attraction is well worth a visit and covers both technological advances and the history of the bridge itself, as well as the river Thames.

There is no charge to walk across the bridge.

Fun Fact: The stone cladding on the outside of the bridge's structure is used to make it appear older than it actually is and for it to blend with the Tower of London's 900-year-old walls. The structural support columns are actually made of steel.

Museum of London

 St. Paul's and Barbican

 £ Free

 Daily from 10:00 to 18:00. Closed 24th to 26th Dec.

 museumoflondon. org.uk

 150 London Wall, EC2Y 5HN

The Museum of London is the perfect place to get an insight into how London has evolved over the last 2000 years.

Here you can see how the city has changed from a Roman settlement to a place with almost 9 million residents.

Learn about the Plague, the Great Fire of London, the Victorian expansion, and much more along the way. Plus, learn about the London that was before the Romans got here.

This is one of our favourite museums in London and the permanent collection is fascinating. Without exception, all temporary exhibitions (most are paid admission) we have seen here have been of very high quality.

Guildhall Art Gallery

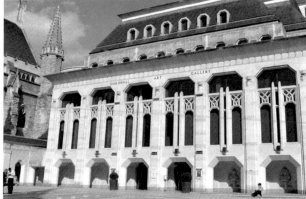

 St. Paul's

 £ Free

 Mon to Sat 10:00 to 17:00, and Sun 12:00 to 16:00.

 bit.ly/guildhallart

 Guildhall Yard, EC2V 5AE

Established in 1885, the Guildhall Art Gallery contains paintings showing London's past; some date as far back as the 1670s. Linked to the art gallery is London's Roman Amphitheatre which dates back almost 2000 years – the remains can be seen here today.

The permanent art collection is free admission, as is entry to the Roman Amphitheatres.

St. Paul's Cathedral

 St. Paul's

 Ad: £18, Conc: £16, Ages 6 to 17: £8, Family: £44

 Mon to Sat 8:30 to 16:30. No tours on Sun.

 stpauls.co.uk

 St. Paul's Churchyard, EC4M 8AD

Sir Christopher Wren's grandest church, St. Paul's Cathedral is an architectural masterpiece. Measuring 365-feet tall and situated on the top of Ludgate Hill – the highest point in the City of London – St. Paul's can be seen from much of the surrounding area.

At the top is the Golden Gallery (528 steps up) where visitors can get an incredible view of central London – you can look west towards Westminster and the London Eye, to the north is the Barbican Centre, east reveals The City and its impressive skyscrapers, as well as

Tower Bridge, whilst to the south you can see The Shard, Shakespeare's Globe Theatre and The Tate Modern.

As well as the viewing area at the Golden Gallery, the Stone Gallery further down provides a good view. Other areas of note include The Crypt, the interior dome, and the Geometric Staircase.

Multimedia guides are included in admission fee, and there are regular guided tours. The most comprehensive guided tour lasts 90 minutes and enters areas not usually open

to the public. You should allow 1.5 to 2 hours to see the church in its entirety, including climbing to the top.

Those wishing to worship can enter the church during services at no cost, but will not be able to enter the visitor galleries or climb to the top – tickets must be shown to do this.

Top Tip: On Sundays, you can enter and briefly see the Cathedral inside without paying. Only a small part of the nave is accessible and there is no touring on this day.

The Bank of England Museum

 Bank

 Free

 Mon to Fri 10:00 to 17:00. Closed on weekends.

 bankofengland.co.uk

 Threadneedle Street, EC2R 8AH

This museum, located inside the Bank of England itself, is filled with things to see. Learn about the 300 years of the Bank's history,

pick up a gold bar, learn about how fraud is reduced through advanced security systems on bank notes, learn about the workings

of the economy, and much more. This is a great museum for people of all ages and contains a variety of interactive exhibits.

The Monument to the Great Fire of London

 Monument

 Ad: £4.50, Conc: £3, Under 16s: £2.30

 9:30 to 17:30 daily Oct to Mar. Late closing at 18:00 Apr to Sep.

 themonument.info

Fish St Hill, EC3R 8AH

The Monument, at 202 ft (62m) tall is the tallest free-standing stone column in the world. It was created to commemorate the Great Fire of London in 1666 and it is located at the northern end of London Bridge.

The Monument contains a narrow staircase with 311 steps, which you can climb for a view of the city. You do have to be in decent physical shape to make it to the top – it is not suitable for those who suffer from claustrophobia. A mesh safety cage restricts the view slightly at the top.

On the way out of The Monument, you are given a certificate with detail about the Fire. Cash only.

Read the inscriptions at the base of the column which describe events: the south side describes King Charles II's actions following the fire, the east side describes how the fire started, and the north side contains a description of the damages caused by the fire.

Sky Garden

 Monument

 Free

 Mon to Fri 10:00 to 18:00, Sat & Sun 11:00 to 21:00. Restaurants & bars open to 1:00 on some nights.

 skygarden.london

 20 Fenchurch St, EC3M 8AF

The Sky Garden at 20 Fenchurch Street, also known as the walkie-talkie due to its peculiar shape, is one of the most impressive free things to do in London.

The Sky Garden is a viewing gallery 35 floors above central London, with a huge inside area filled with plants. It is much more spacious than The Shard across the road, and also includes a small outside area. There's also the added advantage that you can get photos of The Shard itself, and you are closer to the city including the Tower of London and St. Paul's. We actually prefer this view to that from The View from The Shard's gallery.

The Sky Garden is not just a viewing gallery, however, with three food and drink venues – Sky Pod Bar, Darwin Brasserie and Fenchurch Restaurant. Here you can dine, or enjoy a drink, and watch the world go by.

Free tickets are limited to the gallery and are available to be booked three weeks in advance on the website. During peak periods, these dates sell out very quickly. You must bring a valid form of ID to enter Sky Garden.

Eat

Angler
Tube: *Moorgate*
Website: *anglerrestaurant. com*
Phone: *0203 215 1260*
Address: *South Place Hotel, EC2M 2AF*
Hours: *Lunch - Mon to Fri 12:00 to 14:30. Dinner - Mon to Sat 18:00 to 22:00. Closed on Sun.*

Voted one of the top 75 restaurants in London, Angler is a Michelin-starred fish-lover's fantasy. The food is exceptionally presented and deliciously seasoned. The winter terrace offers beautiful views of the city year-round.

Angler is on the pricier end of the scale with a la Carte dishes ranging for £19.50 to £38.50. A three-course lunch menu is available for £35. A 10-course tasting menu is £85. Reservations are recommended.

Polo Bar
Tube: *Liverpool Street*
Website: *polo24hourbar. co.uk*
Phone: *0207 283 4889*
Address: *176 Bishopsgate, C2M 4NQ*
Hours: *Open 24/7*

Whatever time of day you visit, Polo Bar is happy to feed you.

Polo Bar is a café and bar style environment, and serves comfort food in generous portions. Its industrial – yet spotless – interiors show how the area has become gentrified since it first opened in 1959.

Breakfast is served all day and priced at £7 to £10. Lunch and dinner classics are £8.50 to £12, and there is even a budget afternoon tea here for under £10.

Byward Bar and Kitchen
Tube: *Tower Hill*
Website: *thekitchenattower. com*
Phone: *0207 481 3533*
Address: *Byward Street, All Hallows by the Tower, EC3R 5BJ*
Hours: *Mon to Wed 8:00 to 17:00, Thurs and Fri 8:00 to 20:00, Sat 9:00 to 20:00 and Sun 9:00 to 17:00.*

This is one of our favourite gems in the area for well-priced eats. Located on the grounds of All Hallows by the Tower Church (parts of which date back to 700AD), The Kitchen serves British fare in leafy surroundings, and with friendly service that makes you feel like a local.

The tasty English breakfast is £8.90, and most meals are priced at under £14.

Stay

DoubleTree by Hilton – Tower of London
Tube: *Tower Hill*
Website: *doubletree3.hilton. com/en/hotels/united-kingdom/LONTLDI/*
Phone: *0207 709 1000*
Address: *7 Pepys Street, EC3N 4AF*

This modern 4-star hotel is well-located near the Tower of London, but is set far back enough from the busy road to effectively reduce any noise. Considering its location in the heart of The City, it provides great value

for money for a mid-range hotel.

With a 24-hour fitness centre (but no pool), a stunning rooftop restaurant bar, and spacious rooms, we are big fans of this location. The hotel even has Europe's tallest green wall in the lobby. Rooms from £138.

Threadneedles, Autograph Collection by Marriott
Tube: *Bank*
Website: *hotelthreadneedles.co.uk*
Phone: *0207 657 8080*

Address: *5 Threadneedle Street, EC2R 8AY*

Located in a former bank from the 1850s, this 5-star boutique hotel has beautiful, modern interiors and guest rooms, plus classical touches. Service is excellent and personable; it is a small location with only 66 rooms and 8 suites.

The hotel does not have a gym, but provides passes to one nearby.

Rooms from £212.

London Bridge

The London Bridge area is located around the famous bridge and the busy train station on the south side of the river. There are many different things to see and do: the tallest building in Western Europe – The Shard; Shakespeare's Globe Theatre; and the Tate Modern. The current London Bridge is also available for your viewing pleasure, and Borough Market has delicacies to savour year-round.

See and Do

London Bridge

London Bridge and Monument	London Bridge, EC4R 9EL	24/7 - Public Area

Up until the opening of Westminster Bridge in the 1860s, this was the only bridge to cross the river in central London. As such, it has gained somewhat of a mythical status, with several variations of the bridge having existed since the Romans settled 2000 years ago.

From timber bridges, to stone and now a steel and concrete structure, this bridge has always been a vital crossing for the city.

The current bridge dates from 1974 and is a shadow of its former self - previously when the river was three times wider at this point, the bridge span was much larger.

At the northern end of the bridge is The Monument to the Great Fire of London, with The Shard positioned on the other end.

The bridge has even inspired a nursery rhyme – "London Bridge is Falling Down". It

is thought the song comes from the Viking attack in the early 11th century when the bridge was destroyed.

Today's London Bridge is not the best-looking bridge in the city but it is a fantastic place to get perfectly framed photos looking down the river towards Tower Bridge and HMS Belfast, and it vitally connects the City of London with Southwark.

The View from The Shard

 London Bridge

 Ad: £30.95, Conc: £23.95 to £25.95, Ages 4 to 15: £26.95

 29th Oct to 21st Mar: Sun to Wed 10:00 to 19:00, and Thurs to Sat 10:00 to 22:00. 22nd Mar to Oct: 10:00 to 22:00.

 theviewfromthe shard.com

 Railway Approach, SE1 9SG

The Shard is an impressive structure. Standing at 1016 feet (310m) tall, it dominates London's skyline, and is the tallest building in the Western Europe. Towards the top of The Shard (244m up) is a viewing gallery. From here you can to see up to 40 miles away.

The experience starts as soon as you step foot in the building with the "kaleidoscopic" lifts transporting you to Level 69 in seconds. At the top you can explore the city from the indoor levels, or carry on up to the outdoor viewing platforms at Level 72 to get a true sense of how high up you are.

A complimentary multimedia guide and high-tech telescopes tell you about the history of the area, as well as details about key buildings and structures you can see today.

We have to admit, the views from the top are simply stunning and really give you a scale of London. It is a very impressive experience and feels very premium – the sense of being so high up is unlike anything else in the city.

Uniquely, they even offer a "London Landmarks Guarantee", which allows you to return within 3 months if you can't see

certain major monuments during your visit for weather-related reasons.

As well as the standard single entry ticket, The View from The Shard also offers a "Day & Night" ticket with one visit at daytime, and again once the sun has set. This ticket is an upcharge of £10 from standard tickets.

Tickets for The View from The Shard are based on a 30-minute entry time slot. Once at the top, you can spend all long as you want admiring the view. Allow 45 minutes to an hour for the full experience. Book your tickets online to save time and money.

Tate Modern

 London Bridge and Southwark

 Free

 Daily 10:00 to 18:00. Late closing at 22:00 on Fri & Sat. Closed 24th to 26th Dec.

 tate.org.uk/visit/tate-modern

 Bankside, SE1 9TG

Located in an old power station, the Tate Modern features a variety of permanent and temporary modern art exhibitions from around the world.

This is an interesting museum that deserves a few hours of your time, and there is always something new and thought-provoking to see.

The museum's displays are free, but temporary exhibitions are paid admission.

A large extension to the New Tate Modern opened in 2016 with 60% more exhibition space.

Top Tip: Head to the top floor of the new part of the building for an incredible view over the city. There are only four lifts that take you to the 10th floor viewing gallery and waits can be very long - take the stairs instead from the 4th floor if you can.

HMS Belfast

 London Bridge

 Ad: £16, Ages 5 to 15: £8, Family: £27.20 to £47.60, Conc: £12.80.

 10:00 to 17:00 Nov to Feb, 10:00 to 18:00 Mar to Oct

 iwm.org.uk/visits/hms-belfast

 The Queen's Walk, SE1 2JH

Learn all about WWII by stepping aboard a real ship used in the D-Day Landings. You can explore the nine decks of the ship, including the operations room, the living areas, engine rooms, missile rooms and much more.

The ship dates from 1938 and is a big hit, particularly with children. Allow at least two hours to see everything and to engage in the interactive exhibitions, as well as the live demonstrations and talks.

The London Bridge Experience & The London Tombs

 London Bridge

 Ad: £19.95, Ages 5 to 15: £16.50. Fast Pass also available.

 thelondonbridgeexperience.com

 2 Tooley Street, SE1 2SY

 Daily 10:00 to 17:00, with a late closing on weekends at 18:00 and in summer.

These two attractions take you back through London's horrible histories. The "London Bridge Experience" section of the tour is educational, with live guides covering London Bridge's history, ghosts, prisons, war, the Great Fire of London, and Jack the Ripper.

Then, you enter the "London Tombs" section, which is an altogether different experience. This is more like a horror maze type experience where the learning stops and the fear seems to never end as live actors make your experience one to remember.

Compared to the London Dungeon, which we covered earlier in this guide, this is a much less family-friendly experience in the Tombs section. It is much more like a traditional haunted house style attraction in the second part.

The first Experience section is educational; however, we do not recommend this attraction for young children.

Occasionally after hours' events are also offered. These are designed to be even more terrifying than the daytime shows.

Audio guides are available for international visitors to aid them with understanding the historical part of the attraction.

The Millennium Bridge

The Millennium Bridge links The City of London (and St. Paul's Cathedral) with the Tate Modern and Shakespeare's Globe Theatre at Bankside across the river Thames.

The bridge is nicknamed the "Wobbly Bridge" due to an engineering oversight when it was first unveiled. As people crossed the bridge, their walking patterns caused the bridge to sway. It had to be closed only 2 days after opening to fix this issue, and re-opened two years later. Today, it doesn't move and is perfectly safe to cross.

Southwark, St. Paul's and Mansion House	105 Queen Victoria St., EC4V 4ER	24/7 - Public Area

The bridge allows you to get beautiful photos looking down the river towards Tower Bridge.

Harry Potter fans may recognise the bridge as having been destroyed by Death Eaters in the sixth Harry Potter film.

Shakespeare's Globe Exhibition & Tours

 Southwark

 Adults: £15, Conc: £11.50 to £13.50, Ages 5 to 15: £8.

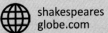 Daily 9:00 to 17:00. Closed 25 & 26 Dec.

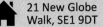 shakespeares globe.com

21 New Globe Walk, SE1 9DT

Explore this faithful reconstruction of Shakespeare's Globe Theatre, opened in 1997, and designed to look as close to the original 1599 Globe as possible.

Inside you can enjoy live Shakespearean shows, explore the exhibition, and tour the building.

The exhibition allows you to learn more about the Bard himself, including where he lived and who he wrote for. You also get an insight into the original Globe's construction and use.

An audio guide is available for the exhibition in several different languages, and is included in the entry cost.

The tours of the building explore the concept of the original Globe, the reconstruction, and its life as a busy, real working theatre. Excellent tours leave every 30 minutes.

Shows are also available at the Globe. These are covered later in our theatre section. Shakespeare fans should be sure to watch one of these.

Tickets include entry to both the exhibition and tour.

Eat

Vapiano
Tube: *Southwark and London Bridge*
Website: *uk.vapiano.com*
Phone: *0207 593 2010*
Address: *90b Southwark Street, SE1 0FD*
Hours: *Mon to Sat 11:00 to 23:00, Sun 11:00 to 22:00.*

Vapiano is probably our favourite 'budget eat' in central London. Choose your seat wherever you want. Then, go to one of the stations to order your food. You can choose from pizza, pasta or salads – your food is prepared fresh in front of you, to your specification in minutes. For pizzas you are given a pager and can wait at the table until your food is ready.

This place is part-fresh fast food, part-canteen, but with restaurant-like quality. It might not be for everyone, but we love it. Portions are large, the meals are tasty, and prices are fair – the perfect combination. Pastas, risotto and pizzas are £7 to £10.50 for a meal. Salads are £5 to £10.

Our only qualm is that the waits for food can be long, as everything is custom cooked from scratch. Vapiano has two more restaurants in London: in Soho and by Oxford Circus station. No reservations.

Aqua Shard
Tube: *London Bridge*
Website: *aquashard.co.uk*
Phone: *0203 011 1256*
Address: *Level 31 – The Shard, 31 St. Thomas Street, SE1 9RY*
Hours: *Restaurant: Weekdays 7:00 to 23:00, weekends & bank holidays 9:00 to 23:00. Bar: Daily 12:00 to 01:00.*

Have lunch or dinner with a view at Aqua Shard. Food is pricey, but the view, service and the delicious meal make it all worth it.

The breakfast set menu is £29 per person. Lunch is £31 for 2 courses, or £34 for 3. Afternoon tea is £42, or add champagne for £20 extra. Dinner is served a la Carte with mains from £29 to £47, with some more affordable vegetarian options.

The views, as you can imagine, cannot be beaten. Reservations are accepted.

José Pizzaro Tapas
Tube: *London Bridge*
Website: *josepizarro.com/ jose-tapas-bar*
Phone: *0207 403 4902*
Address: *104 Bermondsey Street, SE1 3UB*
Hours: *Mon to Sat 12:00 to 22:15, Sun 12:00 to 17:15.*

This pricey Spanish location features mouth-watering dishes, and food is freshly sourced from the market, meaning that the menu really does change daily. Seating is limited, so turn up early for a spot. Reservations are not accepted.

Stay

Shangri La Hotel at The Shard
Tube: *London Bridge*
Website: *shangri-la.com/ london/shangrila*
Phone: *0207 234 8000*
Address: *The Shard, 31 St. Thomas Street, SE1 9QU*

For a room with a view, look no further than the 5-star Shangri La Hotel inside The Shard. Spanning 19 floors, the 202 guest rooms provide unique views of London's skyline.

An infinity pool, a fitness suite and valet parking are some of the amenities on offer. There are three excellent restaurants and bars within the hotel – LANG, TING, and GONG – the highest bar in London on the 52nd floor. Rooms from £351 per night.

London Bridge Hotel
Tube: *London Bridge*
Website: *londonbridgehotel. com*
Phone: *0207 855 2200*
Address: *8-18 London Bridge St, SE1 9SG*

This 4-star hotel is just moments from The Shard and Borough Market. The interiors are contemporary, and this is one of the few hotels not owned by a major chain. Amenities include an on-site gym with a sauna and the Londinium restaurant.

As well as rooms and suites, serviced two-bedroom apartments are available. Rooms from £144 per night.

Hyde Park, Notting Hill & Bayswater

Hyde Park and Kensington Gardens in central-west London are an oasis in the centre of the city. You could spend an entire afternoon, or longer, in the parks just seeing everything they have to offer.

Surrounding the parks are the affluent areas of Notting Hill, Kensington, Marble Arch, Park Lane and Mayfair there too. All the areas around the parks are also worth exploring for their unique characteristics.

The areas around the north of the parks in Bayswater and Paddington are particularly popular with travellers on a budget due to the amount of "motel" style accommodation in this central area.

See and Do

Portobello Road

Ladbroke Grove, Westbourne Park and Notting Hill Gate	Portobello Road, W10 5TA	🕐 24/7 - Public Area

Located in the heart of Notting Hill, this road is home to the world's largest antique market with over 1,000 dealers.

You can come and visit this location any day of the week for a look at the bright, multi-coloured buildings and shops that are open year round, though

Saturdays are the best days to visit with a lot of extra market activity.

More information later in our shopping section.

Hyde Park and Kensington Gardens

 Marble Arch, Hyde Park Corner, Knightsbridge, Lancaster Gate, Paddington and Queensway

 £ Free

 05:00 to 0:00 for Hyde Park. 06:00 to dusk (16:15 to 21:45) for Kensington Gardens.

 royalparks.org.uk/parks/

Once Henry VIII's hunting grounds, today Hyde Park and Kensington Gardens combine to make the largest royal park in central London, spanning some 625 acres. Today, the two parks blend almost seamlessly and offer many sights.

The Serpentine is the largest man-made lake in London – here you can hire out a pedalo or a rowing boat and drift around the lake. It is truly relaxing.

Boat hire is available from April to the end of October from 10:00 to sunset. The hourly rate is £12 per adult and £5 per child. Those fancying a dip may swim at the park's lido.

A 'Solar Shuttle' also operates around the lake if you want someone else to do the sailing work for you.

For the truly warm days, you can sprawl on the grass or hire out one of the deck chairs to sunbathe.

For the colder months of the year, why not pop into the park's several cafés? Numerous playgrounds and restaurants are dotted throughout the parks too.

The Serpentine Gallery and The Serpentine Sackler Gallery are both free admission and include art, architecture and temporary exhibitions. They are open from 10:00 to 18:00 Tuesday to Sunday.

Other highlights of the parks include The Princess Diana Memorial Fountain, the Diana Memorial Playground, and the Italian Gardens and Fountains in Kensington Gardens, which are worth a visit for their beautiful design.

Many statues, fountains and memorials are also dotted around both parks.

On the western end of the Park you will also find the Royal Albert Hall, as well as Kensington Palace.

Speakers' Corner on the north-east corner of Hyde Park, close to Marble Arch, is also another notable attraction. Here, on Sundays, people will gather to hear others exercise their right of free speech.

You will find people on soapboxes talking about daily life, politics, the media and all manner of other subjects – and you can come and listen, for free of course. Anyone can participate by speaking, or simply watching.

Notting Hill

 Notting Hill Gate

 24/7 - Public Area

Well-known for the 1999 film starring Hugh Grant and Julia Roberts, Notting Hill is every bit as charming in person as it is on the big screen. Every corner of this area holds a surprise, and the houses in this expensive area are simply beautiful.

Each year in August, Notting Hill is home to the world's second-biggest carnival – Notting Hill Carnival – where London's West Indian communities gather to put on a joyous street festival filled with fantastic photo opportunities.

Notting Hill is also very well-known for its shopping. More information is available on this aspect later in the shopping chapter of this guide.

Eat

Locanda Locatelli
Tube: *Marble Arch and Bond Street*
Website: *locandalocatelli.com*
Phone: *0207 935 9088*
Address: *8 Seymour Street, W1H 7JZ*
Hours: *Lunch: Mon to Sun 12:00 to 15:00. Dinner: Mon to Thur 18:00 to 23:00, Fri & Sat 18:00 to 23:30, Sun 18:00 to 22:15.*

Amazing tasting Italian food is the name of the game here. The ambience is great, the food is delicious and the service is very attentive.

Pasta mains run from £18.50 to £22.50, whereas fish or meat dishes are £25 to £33. With a dessert, a drink and tip added in (not to mention a starter), you can easily be looking at £50 per person here.

Reservations are accepted.

Roti Chai
Tube: *Marble Arch and Bond Street*
Website: *rotichai.com*
Phone: *0207 408 0101*
Address: *3 Portman Mews*

South, W1H 6HS
Hours: *Street Kitchen - Mon to Sat 12:00 to 22:30, Sun 12:30 to 21:00. Dining Room - Mon to Sat 17:00 to 22:30.*

Roti Chai, serving Indian fare, operates a dual food concept with a Street Kitchen menu, as well as a more formal Dining Room. Both are equally delicious and cater to different types of dining experience.

Small dishes at the Street Kitchen are all under £5, buns are £6 to £7.50, and curry is £7.50 to £8.50. The Dining Room mains are £12.50 to £16. Reservations are accepted for the Dining Room.

Lowry & Baker
Tube: *Westbourne Park & Ladbroke Grove*
Website: *lowryandbaker.com*
Phone: *0208 960 8534*
Address: *339 Portobello Road, W10 5SA*
Hours: *Mon to Sat 8:00 to 16:00, Sun 10:00 to 16:00*

Lowry & Baker is a popular café, which serves traditional sandwiches and cakes, as well as upscale choices such as "Flageolet beans on toast with spinach and homemade pesto".

The menu changes relatively frequently so there is always something new to try. Cash only.

Hereford Road
Tube: *Bayswater and Notting Hill Gate*
Website: *herefordroad.org*
Phone: *0207 727 1144*
Address: *3 Hereford Road, Westbourne Grove, W2 4AB*
Hours: *Mon to Sat 12:00 to 15:00 & 18:00 to 22:30. Sun 12:00 to 16:00 & 18:00 to 22:00.*

Hereford Road serves delicious food at ridiculously low prices. The weekday set lunch menu is amazing value at £13.50 for 2 courses, or £15.50 for 3 and includes food such as fennel and onglet. A la Carte are £12 to £15.50 all day.

Reservations are accepted.

Stay

Four Seasons Hotel Park Lane
Tube: *Hyde Park Corner and Green Park*
Website: *fourseasons.com/london*
Phone: *0207 499 0888*
Address: *Hamilton Place, W1J 7DR*

This 5-star hotel is located in Mayfair, just minutes from Hyde Park, Green Park, Buckingham Palace and the West End.

Amenities include a full-service spa, 24-hour fitness centre, and a multilingual concierge. A lounge/bar and restaurant complete the offerings, with the afternoon tea being a staple option. Service is exceptional.

One of the unique features of the hotel is the first-come, first-served Rolls Royce chauffeur service within a 2-mile range of the hotel. Rooms from £450 per night.

Park Grand London Paddington
Tube: *Paddington and Lancaster Gate*
Website: *parkgrandlondon.co.uk*
Phone: *0207 298 9800*
Address: *1-2 Queen's Gardens, W2 3BA*

This 4-star hotel boasts modern interiors and, in our opinion, is great value, with a good location, modern interiors and attractive pricing. The hotel boasts an on-site restaurant and bar location, which is well priced. Most rates include complimentary breakfast and Wi-Fi.

Two tube stations are an 8-minute walk. Rooms from £88 per night.

Stylotel
Tube: *Paddington*
Website: *stylotel.com*
Phone: *0207 723 1026*
Address: *160-162 Sussex Gardens, W2 1UD*

Located just a few minutes from Paddington station, Stylotel is a 3-star ultra-modern budget hotel. It is relatively small, with only 40 rooms, and 8 apartment suites with kitchenettes. The cheapest rooms are compact, but the value for money is excellent as the hotel is modern and well-located (a 15 minute walk will take you to Oxford Street for shopping and dining, for example).

Breakfast and Wi-Fi are included in most rates, and check-in is from 1:00pm, which is handy for those arriving early into London. Rooms start at £72 per night.

Marylebone, Bloomsbury and Camden

Moving north of Oxford Street, you start to enter the areas of Marylebone, Bloomsbury and Camden. There are quite a few mainline railway stations in this area, including Marylebone, Euston, Kings Cross and St. Pancras.

Bloomsbury is an extremely nice area with many publishing houses located here, as well as the British Museum. Marylebone is in prime central London with Madame Tussauds and the Sherlock Holmes Museum being the most well-known attractions here. Camden is a more alternative area known for its punk scene and food market, as well as the Zoo. The punk scene is less obvious here than ever before, however, as the area has been gentrified in recent years.

See and Do

The British Library

 King's Cross St. Pancras

 Free

 bl.uk

 96 Euston Road, NW1 2DB

 Mon to Thurs 09:30 to 20:00, Fri 09:30 to 18:00, Sat 9:30 to 17:00 & Sun 11:00 to 17:00.

The British Library is the official national library of the United Kingdom. According to its number of catalogued items, it is regarded as the largest library in the world.

It contains a collection of over 170 million items in many languages from different sources.

The British Library is not just books - it is stocked with documents in digital and physical form. They include music recordings, databases, stamps, maps, patents, drawings, magazines and more.

This library even contains historical items and manuscripts dating back to 2000 BC, and the Treasures Gallery exhibition contains gems such as pages from the 800-year-old Magna Carta, an important document that states that everyone should be subject to the law (including royals) and also that everyone has the right to a fair trial.

The Treasures Gallery exhibition closes at 18:00 on Mondays, and with the building on all other days.

ZSL London Zoo

 Camden Town
(15-minute walk)

 Adults: £25, Ages
3 to 15: £19.50,
Conc: £22.50

 Daily 10:00
to 16:00, late
closures at 18:00
in the summer.

 zsl.org/zsl-london-
zoo

 Regent's Park,
NW1 4RY

London Zoo is the world's oldest zoo, having opened in 1828. It houses over 19,000 animals of 800 different species.

Whether you want to see seahorses in the aquarium, the lions on their African plains or the reptile enclosure where they filmed scenes from the first Harry Potter film, there is something here for everyone. There are a large variety of shows and talks throughout the day, as well as several dining locations.

The Gir Lion Lodge is a unique opportunity to stay the night inside the zoo. Your stay includes breakfast and dinner, as well as zoo entry for two days and special guided events. Prices from £438 per night.

The British Museum

 Holborn &
Tottenham Court Rd

 Free

 10:00 to 17:30
(Sat-Thurs) & 10:00
to 20:30 (Fri)

 britishmuseum.org

 Great Russell
Street, WC1B 3DG

The British Museum is one of the largest museums in the world, and houses over 7 million artefacts relating to human history and culture. One of the most fascinating items on display is the Rosetta Stone, which was the key to us understanding Egyptian hieroglyphics. The cat mummies are also a must-see, as are the Egyptian sarcophagi, which are also on display.

At this museum you can travel across time from the age of Enlightenment back to the middle-eastern land of Mesopotamia in 6000 BC, and across the world from Italy to Japan.

There are also regular rotating exhibitions, which means that each visit to this magnificent place is different and equally fascinating.

Madame Tussauds

 Baker Street

 Ad: £35, Child: £30

 Varies. From 10:00 to 16:00 off-peak, to 8:30 to 18:00 in peak. Check website.

 madametussauds. com/London/

 Marylebone Road, NW1 5LR

This famous waxwork museum was the first "Madame Tussauds" location in the world.

Marie Tussaud, born in 1761, made wax masks before public executions in France. Just after the French Revolution she brought her collection of masks to England in an exhibition. The attraction moved to its current home in 1884.

Today, Madame Tussauds is where you can find true-to-life wax representations of famous figures throughout history – real and imaginary.

Inside, there is everyone from David Beckham to Lady Gaga, and The Queen to Albert Einstein.

Recent additions include a section with YouTube stars.

A Sherlock Holmes area and Star Wars locations are also available as of late 2017 – these areas are changed up every few years to keep the attraction's offerings fresh. Do note that some sections of the attraction do cost extra to see.

The attraction also includes a scare zone called the Chamber of Horrors, which can be skipped if you wish.

A classic slow-moving taxi ride through the sights of London is a fun end to your journey.

The Sherlock Holmes Museum

 Baker Street

 Adults: £15, Children: £10

 Daily 9:30 to 18:00.

 sherlock-holmes. co.uk

 221b Baker Street, NW1 6XE

221b Baker Street is undoubtedly one of the most famous addresses in the world. Home of the fictional character Sherlock Holmes, you can now visit the museum.

Explore this Victorian house and move from Sherlock's room to Dr. Watson's and keep an eye out for all the items dotted around, which reference parts of the books.

As the location is a regular-sized house, and was not built as a visitor attraction, you will often see a queue outside the building.

The inside will usually take you less than half an hour to see and given the entry price, this may be best suited for only the most devout Sherlock fans.

Regent's Park

 Baker Street and Regent's Park

 Free

 royalparks.org.uk/parks/the-regents-park

 Regent's Park, NW1 4RY

 05:00 to sunset (16:30 to 21:30)

Regent's Park is an oasis in this area of London, spanning 395 acres. Here you will find the Queen Mary's Rose Garden which every spring blooms with 12,000 roses.

In the summer you will find the Open Air Theatre, usually with at least one or two Shakespeare plays a year. The theatre performs from May to September with tickets costing £25 to £60.

To the north of the park, you will find London Zoo.

Behind Regent's Park, you will find Primrose Hill, which provides one of the most spectacular views of London's skyline from the top.

Harry Potter's Platform 9 ¾ & Shop

 King's Cross St. Pancras

 Free

 Daily 05:00 to 01:00 for photo op. Shop: Mon to Sat 8:00 to 22:00, Sun 9:00 to 21:00.

 harrypotter platform934.com

 Kings Cross Station, Euston Road, N1 9AL

Kings Cross station is a beautiful work of architecture. However, it's what is inside the station that counts – for Harry Potter fans at least.

Fans of the Wizarding boy will remember that King's Cross Station (and more specifically Platform 9 ¾) is where the Hogwarts Express departs from.

Due to the success of the films and books, a photo opportunity with a luggage trolley was put in place between platforms 9 and 10. As this was causing congestion on the platforms, the photo op has now been relocated to the left of the large departure boards in the waiting hall.

This is a very popular spot year-round, so there is a queuing system for the photo opportunity - waits can be long (over 30 minutes) at peak times.

You can take your own photos or get a professional paid one done at this location.

To the left of the photo spot is a shop that sells official Harry Potter merchandise – from Hogwarts scarves to wands, and key-rings to copies of the books.

If you are catching a train from here anyway, this can be a fun way to while away a few minutes.

The Wallace Collection

 Bond Street

 Free

 wallacecollection.org

 Hertford House, Manchester Square, W1U 3BN

 Daily 10:00 to 17:00. Closed 24th to 26th Dec.

The Wallace Collection contains some of the most fascinating pieces of art in all of London. The Great Gallery here has been described as "the greatest picture gallery in Europe."

Highlights of the collection include Frans Hals' "The Laughing Cavalier" dating from 1624, Parisian royal furniture from the 1700s, and Ruben's stunning "The Rainbow Landscape" from 1636. Admission is free to all exhibitions, including temporary ones.

Abbey Road Studios

 St. John's Wood

 £ Free

 Crossing: 24/7. Shop: Mon to Sat 9:30 to 17:30, Sun 10:00 to 17:00.

 abbeyroad.com

 3 Abbey Road, NW8 9AY

Visit the famous zebra crossing from The Beatles' Abbey Road album cover and recreate the scene. You are also free to take photos of the outside of the historic Abbey Road Studios, but the inside is a real working studio, closed to the public.

Be sure to visit the excellent Abbey Road shop for some memorabilia.

There's a live web cam at the crossing so you watch others cross when you're at home.

For the most part, drivers are rather accommodating of visitors taking a picture whilst crossing – but, be careful!

London Canal Museum

 King's Cross St. Pancras

 £ Ad: £5, Child: £2.50, Conc: £4, Family: £12.50

 canalmuseum.org.uk

 12 New Wharf Road, N1 9RT

 Tues to Sun 10:00 to 16:30. Late close on first Thurs of month at 19:30. Closed Mon, except bank holiday Mon.

The London Canal Museum tells the story of the creation of London's canals in the late 18th century.

See what the living conditions were like on board the boats, how important they were for cargo, how their use declined, and how they eventually became seen as a form of leisure. You can even learn how locks work with the interactive exhibitions.

The museum's second theme is ice – you can learn how resourceful the Victorians were with it.

The museum runs canal boat trips with commentary through the Islington Tunnel on Regent's Canal. These are an extra £4 per person on top of museum admission, and run on a few dates only – check the website for details. Pre-booking for boat trips is highly recommended.

Eat

Bento Café
Tube: *Camden Town*
Website: *bentocafe.co.uk*
Phone: *0207 482 3990*
Address: *9 Parkway, NW1 7PG*
Hours: *Sun to Thurs 12:00 to 22:30, Fri & Sat 12:00 to 23:00*

For some of the best Japanese food in London, Bento Café in Camden Town is a fantastic option. Mains such as the Salmon Terriyaki and the Ebi Mentaiko are £7.50 to £19. Side dishes are £3 to £7 each. The sushi and sashimi platters are fresh and are a good option to share, whereas the 'all day bento boxes' are great value at £10.50 to £14.

A few doors down is sister restaurant Bento Ramen, which specialises in ramen noodles and dim sum.

Dishoom
Tube: *King's Cross St. Pancras*
Website: *dishoom.com*
Phone: *0207 420 9321*
Address: *5 Stable Street, Kings Cross, N1C 4AB*

Hours: *Weekdays 8:00 to 23:00, with a late closing at midnight on Thurs and Fri. Sat 9:00 to 0:00, Sun 9:00 to 23:00.*

For authentic, delicious Indian fare, there is no better place than Dishoom. Unusually for London, this restaurant is actually open throughout the day, and even serves breakfast!

Cooked breakfasts and naan rolls are £5 to £8.50. For lunch, small plates are £2.50 to £5, grilled dishes are £6.50 to £12, curries are £8 to £9, salads and vegetarian dishes are all under £10.

Select dishes are also available to takeaway from breakfast to 17:00.

As well as this King's Cross location, Dishoom's other restaurants are just off Carnaby Street, in Covent Garden, and in The City.

Reservations are accepted.

Chiltern Firehouse
Tube: *Baker Street*

Website: *chilternfirehouse.com*
Phone: *0207 073 7676*
Address: *1 Chiltern St, Marylebone, W1U 7PA*
Hours: *Weekdays 7:00 to 22:30, weekends 9:00 to 22:30. Brunch on weekends 11:00 to 15:00.*

This old firehouse has now been converted into a luxury hotel, complete with a fantastic restaurant to boot. Nuno Mendes, Michelin-starred chef, heads up the operation.

With a focus on what is in season, the menu changes regularly, and has an American flair. This place is a favourite of London (and international) celebs.

The venue is beautiful, but this premium experience does carry a cost. Portions are not the largest. Mains are £20 to £44 at both lunch and dinner.

Reservations are accepted, and almost a necessity due to popularity.

Stay

St. Pancras Renaissance Hotel
Tube: *King's Cross St. Pancras*
Website: *stpancraslondon.com*
Phone: 0207 841 3540
Address: Euston Road, NW1 2AR

This stunning building has only recently come out of a lengthy refurbishment, now cementing it is a one of London's top 5-star luxury hotels.

The hotel describes itself as combining "Victorian splendour with contemporary style and impeccable service". The building has so much history that it even offers tours by Blue Badge guides at an extra charge.

As far as dining, you are spoilt for choice: with a bar and restaurant, a lounge, a terrace overlooking the train station, and an upscale dining establishment.

An in-house spa adds to the amenities on offer.

Rooms are relatively large, starting at 25 square metres (270 square feet) on the smallest end of the scale. Prices from £189 per night.

Ibis London Euston St Pancras
Tube: *Euston & Euston Square*
Website: *ibis.com/gb/city/hotels-london-v2352.shtml*
Phone: *0207 388 7777*
Address: *3 Cardington Street, Kings Cross, NW1 2LW*

Ibis is a well-known brand that provides well-priced rooms. This particular location is next door to Euston station, and 10 to 15 minute walk from King's Cross and St. Pancras stations.

An in-hotel restaurant and bar provide dining, and as you would expect from a budget brand there is no on-site fitness suite or pool.

Rooms are basic and make good use of the space, though bathrooms are small.

Rooms from £79 per night.

YHA London St. Pancras
Tube: *King's Cross St. Pancras*
Website: *yha.org.uk/hostel/london-st-pancras*
Phone: *0845 371 9344*
Address: *79-81 Euston Road, NW1 2QE*

This is the only hostel we are listing in the guide, as we consider it to be the best in London.

Just a short walk from the tube, YHA London St. Pancras provides basic, but comfortable, beds for a bargain price.

There is a café-bar area that serves light snacks, the staff are friendly and the British Library is across the road.

Single beds start at £16, with private rooms from £59 per night. Family rooms from £55 per night.

Further Afield

Sometimes it is worth going a bit further out of the centre of the city to experience some unique attractions that you just can't get in central London.

Here, we have listed attractions that are worth making the journey outside of the city centre for.

Some attractions are further out than others, but none will require more than a 1 hour journey. Others are just 10 or 15 minutes from central London.

We do not list any restaurants or accommodation options in this section as we do not feel it is worth making a trip out of the centre specifically to dine. It is also much more practical to remain in central London in terms of accommodation, where you can find places to stay in the heart of the action.

See and Do

Kew Gardens and Kew Palace

 Kew Gardens

 Ad: £19, Child: £5, Conc: £16.50.

 Gardens: Open daily (except 24 & 25 Dec) 10:00 to 16:15, & to 19:30 in summer.

 kew.org/visit-kew-gardens

 Royal Botanic Gardens, Kew, Richmond, TW9 3A

Kew Gardens, opened in 1840, contains the largest collection of living plants in the world. With over 30,000 distinct types of plants and over 7 million plant specimens spanning 300 acres, the scale of the gardens cannot be understated.

This UNESCO World Heritage Site features several buildings to explore, plus it boasts a treetop walkway to give you a unique perspective on the woodland below. Tours are offered throughout the day.

Entry to Kew Gardens includes entry to the gardens, plus Kew Palace (built in 1631 as Samuel Fortrey's country abode), the Royal Kitchens and Queen Charlotte's Cottage (a retreat from her 'mad' husband George III).

The Cottage is only open to visitors at weekends and on Bank Holidays from April to September.

Last entry is 30 minutes before closing.

The small Kew Palace is open in the summer season only from April to September - exact dates to be confirmed. Discounts offered in off-season.

Bushy Park and Richmond Park

 Richmond

 Free

 24/7. Richmond Park has limited hours of 7:30 to 20:00 in Nov & Feb. Bushy Park has limited hours in Sep & Nov 8:00 to 22:30, Mon to Fri.

 Richmond, Greater London

Both Bushy Park and Richmond Parks are free to enter, and they feel like you are a world away from a major capital city.

Both parks are huge. Richmond Park spans 2360 acres, whereas Bushy Park measures some 1099 acres.

They are the two largest royal parks in London and are a short walk from each other.

At Richmond Park, you can enjoy the Isabella Plantation which contains exotic plants; wildlife such as 650 wild deer, trees and birds; King

Henry's Mound with views to St. Paul's Cathedral; as well as leisure activities.

At Bushy Park, you can see the Diana Fountain; the tranquil Upper Water Lodge Gardens; the USAAF memorial; wildlife, and more.

Hampton Court Palace

 Hampton Court (National Rail)

 Ad: £20, Child: £10, Conc: £17 & Family: £51.50.

 Nov to Mar: Daily 10:00 to 16:30. Apr to Oct: Daily 10:00 to 18:00.

 hrp.org.uk/ hampton-court-palace

 East Molesey, Surrey, KT8 9AU

Hampton Court Palace is a sight to behold. The current building dates from the late 1600s. Inside, see England's last medieval hall, the Chapel Royal, the Cumberland Art Gallery,

visit William III's State Apartments, and more.

Outside, explore the gardens and enter the maze to try to find your way out.

Individual maze and Garden tickets are available. Prices quoted are for Palace, Maze and Garden combined tickets. Closed 24 to 26 December.

Greenwich

 Cutty Sark (DLR)

 See below for individual sights.

 24/7 – Public area. Museum and attraction hours vary.

 Greenwich, SE10

Greenwich is one of the London's gems that we still think is under-appreciated to this day. Despite being just 20 minutes away from central London on the tube, it still has a very village-like feel to it, with plenty of green space and has fantastic sight-lines of central London.

Although we have listed Greenwich here as one place, there are many things to do in the area. Highlights in this area include the National Maritime Museum, Cutty Sark, Queen's House and Old Royal Observatory.

The National Maritime Museum is the largest museum of its kind in the world with 10 free galleries to explore. Admission is free.

The Cutty Sark is the world's only surviving tea clipper and dates from the 19th century. You can step aboard the ship and learn all about its history, as well as the restoration work to make it viewable by the public today. Admission is £13.50 per adult and £7 per child.

"The Queen's House" is today used as an art gallery, and dates from the 17th century. Free admission.

The Meridian Line & Historical Royal Observatory at the top of the hill provide spectacular views of the city and Canary Wharf. Here you can take a photo with the prime meridian that divides the world's eastern and western hemisphere and is the basis of GMT (Greenwich Mean Time). Admission is £10 for adults and £6.50 for children.

The Astronomy Centre at the Royal Observatory nearby is free admission and contains interactive exhibitions related to the stars and planets.

Finally, the Old Royal Navy College contains beautiful grounds, as well as the Greenwich Visitor Centre, the stunning Painted Hall (which has been described as 'the Sistine Chapel of the UK'- closed for refurbishment until 2019) and the beautifully quaint Chapel of St Peter & St Paul.

All the museums listed here open from 10:00 to 17:00 daily; they are all closed 24th to 26th December.

Greenwich Royal Park surrounds many of the area's museums and is a great place to sunbathe, relax or have a picnic during the warmer months.

One of the more picturesque ways of getting to Greenwich is via a river cruise from central London – allow 20 to 45 minutes for this journey depending on where you start from.

A more economical way of getting to Greenwich is via the Docklands Light Railway (DLR), which provides interesting views along the way – you can get the DLR at Bank or Tower Gateway in central London. The journey takes about 25 minutes.

Queen Elizabeth Olympic Park

 Stratford International and Stratford

 Park: Free. Venues may charge entry.

 Park: Open 24/7. Venues hours vary.

 queenelizabeth olympicpark.co.uk

 Queen Elizabeth Olympic Park, E20 2ST

The Queen Elizabeth Olympic Park is a public park and sports complex in East London. It was built for the Olympic and Paralympic Games held in summer 2012.

It today offers cultural and sports amenities, as well as many outdoor areas.

As well as enjoying the park's open public spaces, there are numerous playgrounds for children, a climbing wall, gardens and riverside walkways, public art displays, cafés, and more.

The Olympic Stadium is a wonder to behold and is right in the centre of the park. Today, it is home to West Ham United Football Club, and British Athletics.

The Velopark, Hockey and Tennis Centre, and the Aquatics Centre allow you to cycle, bat and swim in the same place that Olympians played at a world level. These are all accessible to the public for a charge. Check for times, session dates and pre-requirements online.

The Arcelormittal Orbit, the UK's tallest sculpture, also dominates the skyline in the park and provides an observation deck at 80 metres in height. On a clear day you can see for up to 20 miles. On the way up, you take a lift to reach the top, and, for an additional charge, you can make your descent on the world's tallest and longest tunnel slide, instead of a lift. Tickets for the viewing platform are £12.50 per adult and £7.50 per child. Concessions are £10.50 and families per £34. Add £5 per person to ride the slide.

Check for events taking place at the park online before visiting as these are plentiful throughout the year.

The park is just 15 minutes from central London, yet feels a world away. It is pure tranquillity and you may just be able to spot some well-known monuments in the skyline in the distance, such as The Shard.

Wimbledon Lawn Tennis Museum & Tours

 Southfields and Wimbledon Park

 Museum only - Ad: £13, Child: £8, Conc: £11

 Daily 10:00 to 17:00 or 17:30.

 wimbledon.com/ en_GB/museum_ and_tours/

 Church Road, Wimbledon, SW19 5AE

Tennis fans are in luck with this whole museum dedicated to the great sport. Museum visits include an audio guide, as well as entry to the 3D cinema, and a 10-minute guided tour of Centre Court.

Inside the museum, visitors can see the Championship

Trophies, learn how the game has evolved since 1877, and see how the Victorians dressed when they played. The museum takes about an hour to see.

For those wanting a more in-depth experience, tours are available which last 90 minutes; these also include

museum admission.

More information on watching a game of tennis here is available in the sports section.

Tour Prices: Adults - £25, Children - £15, Concessions - £21

Legoland Windsor

 Windsor & Eton Riverside and Windsor & Eton Central (National Rail)

 Prices depend on season. Price per person: £45 to £60.

 legoland.co.uk

 Winkfield Road, Windsor, SL4 4AY

 Some days in Mar to May, Sept to Nov. Daily June to Aug. 10:00 to 17:00 off-peak & 10:00 to 19:00 peak.

Legoland Windsor is a theme park aimed at kids aged 2 to 12 with over 55 attractions.

Explore Miniland where you can see models of famous UK landmarks; jump on a train or roller-coaster; hop onto a water ride; or battle mummies on an interactive laser shooting ride – all while surrounded by

millions of LEGO bricks!

Legoland closes over winter. See the website for details.

If you fancy a longer visit, there is an on-site Legoland hotel (with its own mini-water park) - this includes 30 minutes early theme park access and a free second day park ticket, as well as other perks.

A VIP theme park experience is available with faster access to rides, digital copies of your photos, free parking and reserved dining.

The London Underground does not serve Windsor, only National Rail trains. From the rail station you will need to either get a local bus or a taxi to the theme park.

Windsor Castle

 Windsor & Eton Riverside or Windsor & Eton Central (National Rail)

 Ad: £21.20, Conc: £19.30, Ages 5 to 16 or Dis: £12.30, Family: £54.70

 Daily 9:45 to 17:15 Mar to Oct. Nov to Feb, closes 1h earlier.

 royalcollection. org.uk/visit/ windsorcastle

 Windsor, SL4 1Nz

If you are going to make a trip to one castle outside of central London, be sure to make it Windsor Castle. This is the oldest and largest inhabited castle in the world and it is a magnificent sight to behold.

Windsor Castle is where The Queen spends a substantial amount of her time, including many weekends, and a month over the Easter period. To this date the castle has been home to 39 monarchs, spanning back over 900 years.

Your visit to Windsor Castle will include: The State Apartments where the Royal Family often host events for organisations they support; Queen Mary's Dolls' House, the largest doll's house in the world made on a scale of 1:12; The Semi-State Rooms (open from September to March only); and St. George's Chapel.

In the same vain as at Buckingham Palace, there is also a Changing the Guard ceremony at Windsor Castle. The ceremony takes place at 11:00 within the Castle grounds Mondays, Wednesdays, Fridays and Saturdays, but there may be occasional changes to this schedule. A provisional schedule is available online.

Be sure to take in one of the Precinct Tours, led by the Wardens, which last 30 minutes and give you an overview of the castle's history.

A multimedia tour handset can be picked up near the entrance to guide you through the castle – this is available in nine different languages, including English.

A special child-friendly multimedia tour option is also available in English only.

Warner Bros. Studio Tour London – The Making of Harry Potter

 Watford Junction

 Ad: £39-£41, Child: £31-£33, Family: £124-£132

 10:00 to 18:00 in low season, 09:00 to 22:00 in high season.

 wbstudiotour.co.uk

 Studio Tour Drive, WD25 7LR

Harry Potter fans should make The Warner Bros Studio Tour a must-see attraction during their visit, where you can behind the scenes at the studio that made the famed films.

Inside, you will step foot into the Great Hall, see Hagrid's Hut, see wizarding wands, see the real Hogwarts Express and a scale model of Hogwarts Castle, visit Diagon Alley and other film sets, see props and costumes, and much more.

There are both inside and outside sections on this tour, and you will need at least three hours to get a good overview of everything inside.

You can either guide yourself or use one of the multimedia guides, which are available at an additional charge. We recommend guiding yourself.

If you are using public transport to reach this attraction, you can use the Overground to Watford Junction (slow option - 40 minutes) or the fast National Rail train with London Midlands (fast option - 20 minutes). Both depart from Euston National Rail Station. You can use Oyster Cards on both and pricing is the same - £5.30 off-peak and £8.30 at peak times.

From Watford Junction, a regular shuttle bus service runs to the Studios at a cost of £2.50 return per person - cash only.

Alternatively, there is also a shuttle bus service available directly from central London – more information can be found online. If you are arriving by car, parking is free.

Tickets for this attraction must be bought in advance and are not available for purchase on-site. You will select an entry time slot before arrival. All tours are pre-booked.

We strongly recommend booking as far in advance as possible as tickets are limited and they do regularly sell out weeks in advance – even during the off-peak season. There are 'saver' and 'standard' tickets depending on the date of your visit. Saver tickets are £2 cheaper.

Shopping

London is a shopping capital, and British brands sell well around the world. As you can imagine, no matter where you turn in London, you will find somewhere to indulge in some retail therapy. Whether you are looking for luxury items in Knightsbridge or Mayfair, or high street shopping on Oxford Street, you are sure to find something that suits your taste.

Camden Market

🚇 Camden Town   🕐 Daily from 10:00 to 18:00

Camden Market is one experience that visitors to London cannot miss.

From small market stalls to bigger permanent stores, those looking to grab something unique to taste or to take home must make a stop in Camden. If you are a fan of vintage, however, you will get even more joy from your visit!

There are, in fact, six different areas to the market, each with its own character. Explore Inverness Street Market, Stables Market, Camden Lock Market, Buck Street Market, Camden Lock Village and the Electric Ballroom. There are a mix of both indoor and outdoor areas.

The market is most active on Sundays, although trading is also done on Saturdays. A more limited amount of trading takes place on weekdays.

Weekends are definitely the time to visit, however, and the market attracts around 100,000 visitors each and every weekend.

If you are coming for food, you can get this year-round with stalls representing almost every corner of the world.

Oxford Street

 Marble Arch, Bond Street & Oxford Circus and Tottenham Court Road

 Mon to Sat 9:00 to 20:00, Sun 12:00 to 18:00.

Oxford Street is Europe's busiest shopping street (with over half a million visitors daily), and is home to over 300 different stores.

Oxford Street contains all sizes of shop, including many large flagship department stores such as John Lewis, House of Fraser, and Marks and Spencer.

Oxford Street is perhaps most notable for Selfridge's, located to the Western end of the road. Selfridge's, founded in 1909, is the second largest department store in London, after Harrods. It was founded by Harry Gordon Selfridge, an American who coined the phrase 'the customer is always right'.

Also on Oxford Street, you will find brands ranging from United Colors of Benetton to Nike Town and Primark.

New Bond Street and Old Bond Street run perpendicular to Oxford Street; these are the main luxury shopping roads in London, with big international brands, as well as London corporations.

Measuring 1.2 miles (just under 2km) in length, you can spend an entire day on this one road alone.

Hours listed in this section are general shopping hours, with many large shops staying open later until 21:00 or 22:00 from

Monday to Saturday.

Due to Sunday trading laws, large shops can only open for six hours on Sundays. Smaller shops on Oxford Street may still be open later than 18:00 on Sundays.

Starting in Summer 2018, Oxford Street will begin being pedestrianised. The first phase will be completed by December 2018 and the second phase one year later. Taxis will drop you off in the adjacent side streets, but this is an even better reason to use public transport to get to and from Oxford Street.

Regent Street

 Oxford Circus and
Piccadilly Circus

 Mon to Sat 9:00 to 20:00, Sun 12:00 to 18:00.

Regent Street is another popular shopping road in central London. It links to Oxford Street at Oxford Circus.

Regent Street was the world's first shopping street, having been built in the 1820s and rebuilt 100 years later. The façades of all the buildings are lined in Portland Stone, with few exceptions. Today, the street is managed by The Crown Estate. It was originally designed for the Prince Regent (who later became George IV).

Today, Regent Street features a winder mix of prices than Oxford Street – here there are affordable stores stood next to the likes of Burberry and

Swarovski. It is, however, not purely a luxury shopping destination in the same way that New Bond Street and Old Bond Street are.

Notable locations on the street include:
• The Apple Store, located near Oxford Circus. This was the largest of the brand's shops in the world up until 2010;

• Hamley's, a toy store established in 1760 in High Holborn as "Noah's Ark". It moved to its current location in the 1880s. Hamley's is seven floors selling all manner of toys. It is the world's oldest and largest toy shop.

• Liberty, just off Regent Street on Marlborough

Street, is a luxury department store. The building's façade is in a beautiful mock Tudor style.

• BBC Broadcasting House is the headquarters of the British Broadcasting Corporation.

Running parallel to the west of Regent Street is Saville Row, the best place to buy tailor-made suits in London.

Carnaby Street runs parallel to the east of Regent Street. Once the heart of fashionable shopping in the Swinging Sixties, the street is still a well-known name. Today, Carnaby Street is pedestrianised and is home to 150 retailers, and 50 dining locations and bars.

Westfield – London (White City) & Stratford City

 Shepherd's Bush, Wood Lane & Stratford

 White City: Mon to Sat 10:00 to 22:00. Sun 12:00 to 18:00. Stratford: Mon to Fri 10:00 to 21:00. Saturday 9:00 to 21:00. Sunday 12:00 to 18:00.

Looking at the rest of this shopping section, you would be forgiven for thinking that London doesn't have indoor shopping centres. However, the prospect of indoor shopping where everything is in one place does indeed exist.

Today, Westfield owns two large shopping centres, on the eastern and western ends of central London. Both are excellent choices for shopping and feature national and international brands. The differentiation between the two shopping centres is minimal.

The London (White City) location features 372 stores over five levels, whereas the Stratford City location features 350 stores over three levels. The Stratford City location is the largest urban shopping centre in Europe.

Both locations feature a multi-screen cinema, and the Stratford City location also has a casino and a bowling alley. In addition, the Stratford City Westfield is directly connected to the Olympic Park.

Although shops close at a set time at both Westfield shopping centres, the restaurants and other entertainment options are open later.

Bicester Village Shopping Outlet

 Bicester Village (National Rail)

 Mon to Wed 9:00 to 20:00. Thurs to Sat 9:00 to 21:00. Sun 9:00 to 19:00, with select shops open from 11:00 to 17:00 only.

This luxury shopping outlet is located in Oxfordshire, about an hour outside of London.

Access can be obtained by taking a direct train from London Marylebone station to Bicester Village station. The journey takes 46 minutes, with return train tickets priced at £25.

Bicester Village (pronounced "bister") houses 131 stores including several of the world's leading fashion brands like Bally, DKNY, Diane Von Furstenberg, Salvatore Ferragamo, Mathew Williamson, Smythson, Anya Hindmarch, Hugo Boss, Church's and many other brands.

There are also dining establishments to take a break between all the shopping.

This is a popular destination and hosts over 6 million shoppers every year. The outlets are open year-round, and are particularly popular on bank holidays.

Knightsbridge and Harrods

Knightsbridge is a luxury shopping and residential district. With Hyde Park on one side, and Belgravia to the other, Knightsbridge is perfectly placed in the lap of luxury.

Notable brands in the area include Ferrari, Harvey Nichols, Rolex, Aquascutum and Porsche Design.

The most well-known store in the area is Harrods. Founded in 1834, this luxury department store is the de facto destination for the rich.

 Hyde Park Corner and Knightsbridge   Harrods: Mon to Sat 10:00 to 21:00. Sun 11:30 to 18:00. Other shops vary.

Harrods is the biggest department store in Europe, with 330 departments and retail space of 1 million ft² (90,000 m²). It is worth exploring to see the incredible variety of extravagant things on offer, and the beautiful food court has to be seen to be believed.

Brick Lane

 Shoreditch High Street and Aldgate East   Shops open daily 9:00 to 19:00. Main market on Sun 10:00 to 17:00.

Brick Lane is a fashionable, up-and-coming destination in Central-East London, and the heart of the British Bangladeshi community. Many call it Banglatown, and it is widely known for its curry houses.

The street got its name from the manufacturing of brick and tile during the 15th century. The area around Brick Lane houses many religious institutions, including Christ Church and Brick Lane's Great Mosque.

Brick Lane is filled with fashionable shops which are open daily, as well as street art including works from Banksy and D*Face. It is also well-known for its nightlife.

Brick Lane Market is a popular destination on Sundays and specialises in second-hand goods, including clothes, furniture, books, and more. Trading here takes place on Sundays from 10:00 to 17:00.

Borough Market

 London Bridge Lunch market only: Mon & Tue 10:00 to 17:00. Full market (incl lunch): Wed & Thurs 10:00 to 17:00. Fri 10:00 to 18:00. Sat 8:00 to 17:00. Closed Sun

Nestled across from London Bridge station, Borough Market is definitely worth a visit for foodies.

The Central London food market is known as one

of the oldest and largest markets in London. It is stocked with food sourced from all the continents of the world.

Borough is steeped in

history. It has been the site of food markets for over 1000 years, but the market on the current site has been present since the 18th century.

Piccadilly

Piccadilly gets its name from the white frilly collars that were once sold in the area – the Piccadills.

Today, Piccadilly is still a commerce street with several unique shops. Many of the shops in the area hold Royal Warrants; these are seals of approval from senior members of the Royal Family who shop there.

Notable locations include:
• **Fortnum and Mason**, established in 1707, with very lavish, classic British interiors it sells luxury goods and has its own tea room.
• **Burlington Arcade** with its small boutique shops is beautiful. The Piccadilly Arcade across the road is similar, yet more simple.
• **Hatchards**, a bookshop that has been present on

 Green Park and Piccadilly Circus Mon to Fri 10:00 to 20:00, Sat 9:00 to 20:00, Sun 12:00 to 18:00.

the road since 1797, is a treasure trove inside and regularly holds high-profile signings.
• **Waterstones** is a modern book shop spanning six floors, with over 200,000 unique titles. This is the largest bookshop in Europe and is open to 22:00 every day, except Sunday. It even

has its own restaurant and bar on the top floor, called 5th view. There is also a café.

The Ritz Hotel and the Hard Rock Café are other well-known locations here.

Times listed are general opening hours and individual shop hours vary.

Notting Hill and Portobello Road

 Ladbroke Grove, Westbourne Park and Notting Hill Gate

 Daily 9:00 to 17:00. The main market is on Saturdays.

Notting Hill is a mostly residential district in London. It is well known for hosting the annual Notting Hill Carnival, and the weekly Portobello Road Market. It is one of London's most affluent areas.

Portobello Market (on Portobello Road) is a street market divided into sections. You will find antiques, fruit and veg, new goods, clothes and fashion, and second hand items sold at the market. The antiques are undoubtedly what the market is most famous for.

The market takes place on Saturdays and starts to get busy from 9:00 onwards, and starts winding down between 17:00 and 19:00.

Some trading at this market does take place on other days of the week, mostly from the permanent shop fronts, but Saturday is *the* day to come.

Covent Garden

Covent Garden is a popular visitor destination, with shopping in every direction you look. The area is in the heart of Theatreland, and ideal for post- or pre-theatre shopping and dining.

Covent Garden started life in 1654 as an open vegetable and fruit market in the southern part of the square.

The pedestrianised square is still the heart of the area but shops are now on all the surrounding streets too. Under the square's central roof, you will find a split-level set of shops with many small boutiques present.

 Covent Garden

 Mon to Fri 10:00 to 20:00, Sat 9:00 to 20:00, Sun 12:00 to 18:00.

Big international brands are also on the square, such as the likes of Apple, Barbour and Chanel.

We love the ambiance of Covent Garden. The times listed are general opening times and individual shop hours vary.

Music, Theatre and Arts

As well as shopping and museums, culture buffs have no shortage of things to do in London either. The West End is the heart of the theatre district with musicals, comedies and dramas galore. If live music is more your scene, that is catered for too. Those wanting to party away into the night will also find solace in London's nighttime scene.

Musicals

Musicals have been a staple in London for years and there is a wide array to choose from.

❶ Matilda: The Musical
Nearest Station: Covent Garden
Website: matildathemusical.com
Run Time: 2 hours and 45 minutes with one intermission
Address: Cambridge Theatre, Earlham Street, WC2 9HU

Matilda: The Musical is based on Roald Dahl's novel of the same name. Matilda has already been turned into a famous film, and now it is a wildly successful musical too.

Matilda on Broadway won seven Olivier awards in 2012; in London this popularity continues. It is easy to see why: with catchy songs, great décors and a story we can all relate to in some way or another, Matilda captures the hearts of theatregoers. A must-watch!

❷ The Phantom of the Opera
Nearest Station: Piccadilly Circus
Website: thephantomoftheopera.com/london
Run Time: 2 hours and 30 minutes with a 15-minute intermission
Address: Her Majesty's Theatre, Haymarket, SW1Y 4QL

An Andrew Lloyd Webber production that tells the tale of a fascinating love story unlike anything you have ever seen before. With incredible scriptwriting, memorable songs and incredible set changes, it is no wonder that this show has now been performing for over 30 years at Her Majesty's Theatre.

❸ Book of Mormon
Nearest Station: Piccadilly Circus
Website: thebookofmormonlondon.com
Run Time: 2 hours 30 minutes with a 15-minute intermission
Address: Prince of Wales Theatre, Coventry Street, W1D 6AS

The Book of Mormon is a satirical musical based on The Church of Jesus Christ of Latter-day Saints. The story follows two Mormon missionaries to Uganda and the struggles they face as AIDS, poverty, war and famine impede their activities. The musical is hilarious, with clever lyrics, and won four Olivier awards in 2014. Beware if you are easily offended - there is a lot of swearing!

❹ Aladdin
Nearest Station: Leicester Square
Website: aladdinthemusical.co.uk
Run Time: 2 hours 30 minutes with one intermission
Address: Prince Edward Theatre, Old Compton St, W1D 4HS

Disney brings its classic film story to life in London with Aladdin, featuring an incredibly funny Genie and all the songs from the film.

The sets, decor and costumes are incredible and the special effects have to be seen the believed. A magical night out!

❺ Les Miserables
Nearest Station: Piccadilly Circus
Website: lesmis.com
Run Time: 2 hours 50 minutes with a 20-minute intermission
Address: Queens Theatre, 51 Shaftesbury Ave, W1D 6BA

Les Miserables is based on the novel of the same name by Victor Hugo. The musical is set in France during the 19th century and recounts the tale of a French peasant named Jean Valiean who seeks salvation after spending nineteen years behind bars. The musical was originally unveiled in French, with its English lyrics later being composed by Herbert Kretzner.

❻ Thriller Live!
Nearest Station: Piccadilly Circus
Website: thrillerlive.com
Run Time: 2 hours and 10 minutes with a 20-min intermission
Address: Lyric Theatre, 29 Shaftesbury Avenue, W1D 7ES

Thriller Live! is a concert-style experience that celebrates Michael Jackson, and the music of The Jackson 5. In 1988, the show started as a fan club based in Britain. The huge following of the show led to an annual tribute concert for Michael Jackson. Now, this is the closest thing to the real deal. There is no acting, it is just song after song.

Though the idea of being seated may seem odd for a concert, by the end of the show you will be up and dancing.

❼ Mamma Mia!
Nearest Station: Covent Garden
Website: mamma-mia.com
Run Time: 2 hours and 35 minutes with a 15-min intermission
Address: Novello Theatre, Aldwych, WC2B 4LD

Mamma Mia is another West End favourite, and retells the story of a bride-to-be who tries to find which of three men is her real father. Of course, all this is just an excuse to get as many ABBA songs into one musical as possible. Tracks include: Dancing Queen, Super Trouper, Take a Chance on Me, The Winner Takes It All, SOS, and a host of others.

8 The Lion King
Nearest Station: Covent Garden
Website: thelionking.com
Run Time: 2 hours and 40 minutes with a 15-min intermission
Address: Lyceum Theatre, 21 Wellington Street, WC2E 7DA

The Lion King is one of the most popular animated movies of all time, and Disney has taken the opportunity to turn it into a musical. The musical made its way to the West End in 1999.

Instead of having people dress up as the film's characters, intricate marionettes and puppets are used to retell the story in a way never seen before.

9 Wicked
Nearest Station: Victoria
Website: wickedthemusical.com
Run Time: 2 hours and 45 minutes with a 15-min intermission
Address: Apollo Victoria Theatre, 17 Wilton Rd, SW1V 1LG

Wicked is the untold story of the Wicked Witch of the West from the popular tale "The Wizard of Oz". Here you discover why the Witch is so mean, and what an amazing story it is. With hilarious songs, a fantastic script and sets to astound, this is one of the best shows we have ever seen.

10 Hamilton
Nearest Station: Victoria
Website: hamiltonthemusical.co.uk
Run Time: 2 hours and 45 minutes with a 15-min intermission
Address: Victoria Palace Theatre, Victoria Street, SW1E 5EA

Hamilton: The Musical is finally making its debut in London after becoming the most difficult to get ticket in New York City. The winner of the Pulitzer prize and 11 Tony awards, Hamilton opens on 6 December 2017.

The musical retells the story of the struggle felt by the Founding Fathers of the USA. Most of the music is set to a clever and funny hip hop-style. This will be *the* ticket to get in 2018.

Drama

❶ The Woman in Black
Nearest Station: Covent Garden
Website: thewomaninblack.com
Run Time: 2 hours with one intermission
Address: Fortune Theatre, Russell Street, WC2B 5HH

The Woman in Black is a horror stage play performed by only two actors. The play follows the story of a lawyer obsessed with a curse that he believes has been cast over him and his family by the spectre of a Woman in Black.

Get ready to be creeped out, as the small theatre adds to tense atmosphere. Having been in London for over 25 years, this is one show that will be terrifying audiences for years to come.

❷ The Mousetrap
Nearest Station: Covent Garden
Website: the-mousetrap.co.uk
Run Time: 2 hours and 15 minutes with a 15-minute intermission
Address: St. Martin's Theatre, West Street, WC2H 9NZ

The Mousetrap, written by Agatha Christie, first opened in 1952 and has been consistently running since then. With over 25,000 performances, and a run time of 65 years, it is the longest running modern play anywhere in the world. In typical Agatha Christie style, this is a case of trying to guess "whodunit".

Theatre-goers are asked not to reveal the ending before leaving the theatre in order to keep the enjoyment for future audiences.

❸ The Play That Goes Wrong
Nearest Station: Covent Garden
Website: theplaythatgoeswrong.com
Run Time: 2 hours and 5 minutes, with a 20-minute intermission
Address: Duchess Theatre, Catherine Street, WC2B 5LA

The Play That Goes Wrong is based on the antics of the Cornley Polytechnic Drama Society who is trying to stage a 1920s murder mystery, and everything that can go wrong, does. With so many genuine laugh out loud moments, it is no wonder that the play won 'Best New Comedy' at the 2015 Olivier awards.

❹ Harry Potter and The Cursed Child
Nearest Station: Leicester Square
Website: harrypottertheplay.com
Run Time: Part 1 is 2h 45m, Part 2 is 2h 35m - shown as separate performances.
Address: Palace Theatre, Shaftesbury Ave, W1D 5AY

The most difficult play to get tickets to - this is a masterpiece, with great acting, a fantastic storyline, incredible sets and magical special effects, Potter fans should not miss out on the opportunity of a lifetime to see what happened to 'The Boy Who Lived' after the films. The story is split into 2 separate performances.

Dance, Opera and Other Performances

❶ Shakespeare Globe Theatre
Nearest Station: London Bridge and Southwark
Website: shakespearesglobe.com
Address: 21 New Globe Walk, SE1 9DT

Shakespeare's Globe Theatre is a recreation of the magnificent, original Globe Theatre. The current building stands around 230 metres from the original structure. Ever since it was reopened in 1997, the Shakespeare Globe Theatre has staged plays every summer. Tours of the building are also available.

❷ London Coliseum (English National Opera)
Nearest Station: Leicester Square
Website: eno.org
Address: St Martin's Lane, WC2N 4ES

The London Coliseum is a theatre situated at St. Martin's Lane in Central London. It was constructed as one of the most luxurious and largest variety theatres in London, and opened in December 1904. Today it is primarily used for opera, as well as being the London home of the English National Opera.

❸ Royal Opera House
Nearest Station: Covent Garden
Website: roh.org.uk
Address: Bow Street, WC2E 9DD

Situated in Covent Garden, the Royal Opera House is a venue used for various types of performing arts. It houses several groups like The Royal Ballet, The Orchestra and The Royal Opera. It was originally called the Theatre Royal and served as a playhouse for the first century of its history. Tours are available.

❹ The Roundhouse
Nearest Station: Chalk Farm
Website: roundhouse.org.uk
Address: Chalk Farm Road, NW1 8EH

The Roundhouse is an old railway engine shed located in Chalk Farm. Just before World War II, the building fell into a state of disuse. In 1964, it was reopened as a venue for performing arts.

After being empty for years, performing arts returned to this building after it was purchased by a local businessman in 1996. It is now one of the most unique venues in London with a capacity of 1,700 people.

Live Music and More

● The O2 Arena
Nearest Station: North Greenwich
Website: theo2.co.uk
Address: Peninsula Square, SE10 0DX

Initially called the Millennium Dome, The O2 is an arena with a seating capacity of 20,000, as well as a dining venue with a cinema. It is one of the main music venues in London, and has the second highest capacity in the UK, after The Manchester Arena. It is the world's busiest arena by a large margin, with 1.8 million ticket sales in 2015.

The easiest way to reach the venue is by tube (North Greenwich station) on the Jubilee Line, with a travel time of only 15 minutes from Central London. Another popular option is the Thames Clippers River Express from river piers in Central London.

❷ Wembley Arena
Nearest Station: Wembley Park
Website: ssearena.co.uk
Address: Arena Square, Engineers Way, HA9 0AA

Once a swimming pool, Wembley Arena is now a premiere music venue located right next to the behemoth Wembley Stadium. It is the second largest indoor arena in London, after the O2, with 12,500 seats. It features good transport links, and is located only half an hour from central London.

❸ Royal Albert Hall
Nearest Stations: South Kensington, Gloucester Road and High Street Kensington
Website: royalalberthall.com
Address: Kensington Gore, Kensington, SW7 2AP

The Royal Albert Hall is a multi-purpose concert hall in South Kensington. The Hall has a seating capacity of almost 5,300 for performances by rock bands or pop stars, ballets or operas.

The building dates from 1871, when Queen Victoria and Prince Edward opened it. It has been the residence concert venue for The BBC Proms every summer since 1941; these are daily classical music performances, usually at affordable prices.

As well as the large, paid events in the main hall, there are also Free Music Fridays. These take place in Verdi, the Italian restaurant within the building – a different artist, or series of artists, plays every week.

Tours of the building are also available; more information on this is available in the neighbourhood guide section of this book.

4 Barbican Centre
Nearest Station: Barbican
Website: barbican.org.uk
Address: Silk Street, EC2Y 8DS

The Barbican Centre is a performing arts centre and the largest of its kind in Europe. The Centre hosts classical and contemporary music concerts, theatre performances, film screenings and art exhibitions.

The Barbican Hall is home to the London Symphony Orchestra and the BBC Symphony Orchestra. The interiors are pleasant and there is always something different going on, but be sure to check what is showing in advance before visiting to avoid disappointment.

5 The British Film Institute (BFI) Southbank
Nearest Stations: Waterloo
Website: bfi.org.uk
Address: South Block, Belvedere Rd, SE1 8XT

A four-screen cinema venue showing over 2,000 classic and contemporary films each year, with film seasons, director and actor retrospectives, and extended runs of cinema classics. View over 1000 hours of free film and TV in the Mediatheque, visit the library and film shop, and enjoy two of the Southbank's best restaurant bars. The BFI National Archive, the largest film archive in the world contains 150,000 movies and around 625,000 television programs.

Pricing is: Adults - £12.10, Concessions 0 £9.70, Children (Under 16) - £6. If you are 25 or under and register online, you can get tickets for just £3 with valid ID.

6 Southbank Centre
Nearest Station: Waterloo
Website: southbankcentre.co.uk
Address: Belvedere Road, SE1 8XX

The Southbank Centre is a 21-acre estate running from County Hall to Waterloo Bridge, and is Europe's largest center for the arts.

The Royal Festival Hall is a world-renowned concert hall for music, dance and literature.

The Hayward Gallery features visual arts across all periods and has a very diverse set of exhibitions. Past shows featured works of Leonardo da Vinci, Eduard Munch and French Impressionists.

The Southbank Centre welcomes a wide range of creativity – music, arts, classical, rock, pop, jazz, dance, yoga, performances, spoken word, poetry, visual arts, painting, sculpture, architecture, and more. There are four resident orchestras: London Philharmonic Orchestra, Philharmonic Orchestra, Orchestra of the Age of Enlightenment, and London Sinfonietta.

The Queen Elizabeth Hall, Purcell Room and Hayward Gallery will be closed until some time in 2018 for refurbishments.

Nightlife

London has a thriving nightlife scene! From relaxing bars, to pubs to spend a few hours, to the pounding music from the club nights, London's character changes after the sun sets, and the partying goes on into the early hours of the morning in many locations.

Bars

❶ Opium
Nearest Station: Leicester Square
Phone: 0207 734 7276
Website: opiumchinatown.com
Address: 16 Gerrard Street, W1D 6JE

Pop in for the best dim sum in town, and creative cocktails with Asian-inspired ingredients. Expect to pay £11 to £15 for a cocktail here and £5 to £6 for a beer.

❷ Vista at The Trafalgar
Nearest Station: Charing Cross
Phone: 0207 870 2900
Website: thetrafalgar.com/vista-homepage/
Address: 2 Spring Gardens, Trafalgar Square, SW1A 2TS

The name says it all here: Vista. It is the view you come for when visiting this rooftop bar overlooking Trafalgar Square. This is a seasonal venue that operates during Spring and Summer, and serves light food. There is a £5 cover charge for this venue, and a minimum spend.

It is also usually opens on the 31st December to ring in the New Year and see the fireworks when a pricey private event operates.

❸ Cahoots
Nearest Station: Piccadilly Circus and Oxford Circus
Phone: 0207 352 6200
Website: cahoots-london.com
Address: 13 Kingly Street, W1B 5PG

Cahoots is one of our favourite themed bars with the interiors resembling an old Underground train and even the staff are in character. There are a wide variety of cocktails on offer, which are all fantastic, and they usually host live music acts. This is a popular location and table reservations (for a 2-hour slot) are a must.

Clubs

❶ Koko
Nearest Station: Mornington Crescent
Website: koko.uk.com
Address: 1a Camden High Street, NW1 7JE

This Camden club is popular because of its affordable entrance prices, large selection of acts, and interesting layout inside. It was once a theatre and you can tell as soon as you step in the venue. We are not huge fans of the prices charged for drinks, however!

The venue hosts regular events other than standard club nights, such as concerts throughout the week. There are very few places to rest, though, so be prepared to stand. If you do need to sit down, look out for the leather sofas at the back of the main room.

❷ The Electric Ballroom
Nearest Station: Camden Town
Phone: 0207 485 9006
Website: electricballroom.co.uk
Address: 184 Camden High Street, NW1 8QP

A well-known venue in London, The Electric Ballroom provides well priced drinks, a fantastic ambiance, and regular national and international acts. It comes highly recommended for a night out and has a good balance between a club and music venue. The top area has seats for those wanting to chill out for a bit.

❸ Fabric
Nearest Station: Farringdon and Barbican
Phone: 0207 336 8898
Website: fabriclondon.com
Address: 77a Charterhouse Street, EC1M 6HJ

Fabric is a well-known nightclub in London, and is extremely popular so get there early. This is a place for people who really like their music and will appreciate the fantastic sound system. Expect to pay at least £20 for entry – sometimes closer to £30, but they regularly get big name DJs. Book your tickets in advance, if you can, to reduce your wait getting in.

Pubs

❶ The Lock Tavern
Nearest Station: Chalk Farm and Camden Town
Website: lock-tavern.com
Phone: 0207 482 7163
Address: 35 Chalk Farm Road, Camden

This pub is well-sized, with a large beer garden and roof terrace, which makes it perfect for a sunny day. Food is generally good, and drink prices are acceptable for the location. There are occasional live music acts too, which also add to the ambiance.

❷ Ye Olde Cheshire Cheese
Nearest Station: Chancery Lane and St. Pauls
Phone: 0207 353 6170
Address: 145 Fleet Street, EC4A 2BU

If you want history and ambiance, there is no better pub to pay a visit to in The City. This pub was rebuilt in 1667 and stepping foot inside is like going back 350 years.

Go downstairs into the authentic drinking areas deep underground and be reminded how much shorter people were as you duck down the steps. We love the ambiance inside, and the food and drink are decent too! Even Samuel Johnson used to drink here!

❸ The Cross Keys
Nearest Station: Covent Garden
Phone: 0207 836 5185
Website: crosskeyscoventgarden.com
Address: 31 Endell Street, WC2H 9BA

An absolutely tiny, intimate location that is very pretty inside (and outside). Beer and food are good. Get there early for a table or seat. It is conveniently located in the West End so it perfect if you would like to carry on your night in one of the many bars or clubs in the area.

Getting back after a night out
Be aware that most of London's Underground system stops running from the city centre around midnight, with night buses and taxis being the main ways to get around after that. Alternatively, you could party away into the night until the first trains reach the centre of London around 6:00.

On Friday and Saturday nights there are services in a large part of the Central, Northern (Charing Cross Branch), Piccadilly, Victoria and Jubilee Lines, with trains running at 10-20 minute intervals throughout the night. A small section of the Overground also runs.

If you are returning home on a night out in a taxi, either hail a black cab or book a car/mini-cab (by calling or via an app) – hopping into a mini-cab in the spur of the moment is illegal and unsafe. Remember if your car/minicab is not pre-booked, there is no trace of your journey should anything go wrong.

Sport

What better way to round your trip off in London than with a bit of live sport? London has plenty of choice with sporting arenas dedicated to football, tennis, rugby and cricket, as well as multi-use venues.

The best place to get tickets for any sport is to check online at the official stadium websites, which will link to authorised sellers.

Not using the official sales channels, and visiting ticket resellers, may either mean paying too much, getting fake tickets, or both. Many locations also sell tickets directly at the box office on-site.

For tours of the locations featured below you can either pre-purchase tickets online, or (for some) buy them on the day of your visit. Tickets are cheaper in advance, and you can avoid the disappointment of turning up and finding that tours are all sold out.

Stadium tours selling out is relatively common, particularly during summer months and school holidays.

Wembley Stadium

 Wembley Park

 wembley stadium.com

🏠 Wembley Stadium, Wembley, HA9 0WS

Wembley Stadium is a 90,000-seater football stadium in north-west London. It is the largest stadium in the UK, the second largest in Europe, and opened in 2007, replacing the old stadium.

Wembley hosts the FA Cup Final, the England national football team, and other big football matches like the UEFA League.

Be sure to look out for the bronze statue of Bobby Moore at the stadium entrance, which commemorates England's 1966 World Cup win. The stadium is located about 30 minutes from central London by tube or car.

As well as sports events, the stadium has also staged music performances from renowned artists such as Oasis, U2 and Coldplay.

Aside from the matches played here, you can tour the inside of the stadium year-round, except on Wembley event days.

Experience the awesome behind-the-scenes feel and action as your tour guide leads you to the changing rooms, the press conference room, the VIP club for a spectacular panorama of the stadium, the royal box, the exhibitions, and the stadium store.

Tours last 75 minutes and depart hourly from 10:00 to 15:00 and are priced at £20 per adult, £12 per child (under 16), with concessions paying £12. A family ticket is £50. A VIP tour option is also available.

Lord's Cricket Ground

Lord's Cricket Ground is the definitive home of cricket in London, and is situated in St. John's Wood.

Established in 1814, this 28,000-seater venue hosts international test matches and major local competitions.

Lord's is also home to the MCC Museum, which contains the precious Ashes urn from 1882. The present Lord's is the third incarnation.

If you are not visiting for a sporting event, you can still tour the cricket ground year-round. Tour tickets include entry to the museum.

Tours last 100 minutes and run 7 days a week. You will see the Honours Board, sit

St. John's Wood | lords.org | St John's Wood Road, NW8 8QN

in the dressing rooms, enter the Long Room, and of course see the Ashes Urn.

The Lord's Tour is very popular, especially during the summer months, and tours are often fully booked in advance. Prices are £24 for adults, £18 for over 60s,

£15 for children (5 to 15) and students, and £78 for a family. Tours do not run on major match days.

The MCC Museum is open on all match days for visitors with a ticket for that day's play.

Wimbledon

 Southfields and Wimbledon Park | wimbledon.com | Church Road, Wimbledon, SW19 5AE

The best known and oldest Tennis tournament in the world, The Championships at Wimbledon should not be missed by any fans of the sport.

Tickets for games are sold in advance through a

ballot system whereby a computer randomly selects winners, and assigns them a game to watch. In 2018, The Championships run from 2nd July to 15th July inclusive. For 2018 matches, the ballot closes on 15th December 2017.

Wimbledon also runs tours and has a museum. More information on this is available in the neighbourhood guides section of this book, under "further afield".

Emirates Stadium – Arsenal F.C.

The Emirates Stadium is the third biggest football stadium in England with a capacity of 60,272 seats.

The Emirates Stadium is open to visitors year-round through tours, and even has a museum. At the museum you can immerse yourself in the history of Arsenal F.C. by following the story of the club's formation in 1886 right through to the present day. You can also see famous shirts and boots in the exhibition.

Arsenal | bookings.arsenal.com | Hornsey Road, N7 7AJ

Tickets are £10 for adults, £7 for children (under 16) and £8 for concessions.

A self-guided audio tour is another option. Here you can let a host of Arsenal stars share their matchday experiences with you as you explore behind-the-scenes at Arsenal Football Club using audio visual guide handsets. You will explore areas such as the Director's Box, Home and Away Changing Rooms, Players' Tunnel, Pitchside and more.

All tours include free entry to the Arsenal Museum, branded Arsenal headphones and a tour certificate.

Audio tour tickets are £22 per adult, £14 for children (under 16), with family tickets costing £55. Matchday tours and Legend Tours (held by ex-Arsenal players for £40 per person) are other options.

Stamford Bridge – Chelsea F.C.

Chelsea's Stadium, also known as Stamford Bridge, has a 41,798-seat capacity and is located in the affluent area of Fulham in central London.

Stamford Bridge offers a fantastic behind-the-scenes tour of the stadium at £19 per adult and £13 per child. The guided 1-hour tour takes you behind the scenes, visiting various stands in the stadium, the press room, Home & Away dressing rooms, the tunnel and more.

All tours also include entry to the Museum, giving you the chance to see how Chelsea has evolved on and off the pitch to become

Fulham Broadway | chelseafc.com | Fulham Road, SW6 1HS

one of the greatest football clubs in the world.

The tours run daily (but not on match days and other dates – check online), and leave every 30 minutes from 10:00 to 15:00.

Museum-only admission is £11 per adult and £9 per child. Platinum tours, and legends tours are also available at an additional cost. Legends tours with ex-Chelsea players are also available.

The Oval

The Oval Cricket Ground was built in 1845, and in 1880 hosted the first international test match between England and Australia. To this day, the final Test match of the English cricket season is traditionally played here. The Oval has a seating capacity of 23,500.

The Oval was also the location of the first ever international football match in 1870 between England and Scotland.

 Oval   kiaoval.com   The Oval, SE11 5SS

Tours of the Oval are available. During the tour you will step foot in the players' dressing rooms, see where the players train, enter the press box, and access the Corinthian roof terrace with its stunning views of London.

Tours take place on Fridays and Saturdays at 11:00 on non-match days. Additional mid-week tour dates are available around key international fixtures.

A full ground tour lasts

approximately 90 minutes. Tickets are £20 per adult, £10 for children under 16.

If booking in person, The Oval accepts cash only. Tickets may also be pre-booked online.

Twickenham Stadium

Twickenham Stadium is the largest stadium in the world dedicated to rugby union, with a seating capacity of 82,000 people. Opened in 1909, it is mainly a rugby venue, but the stadium has also staged concerts.

Guided tours are available, priced at £20 per adult, £15 for concessions, £12 per child (5 to 15), and £50 for a family ticket.

 Twickenham (National Rail)   englandrugby.com/twickenham   Whitton Road, TW2 7BA

Included in the tour are a visit to the royal box, players' tunnel, a view of the arena from the top of the stand, and a pitchside walk, as well as a visit to the England dressing room. Tours also include entry to the World Rugby Museum.

Museum-only tickets

are £8 for adults, £7 for concessions, £6 for children, and £25 for a family ticket.

Stadium tours are not available on select dates due to matches and events at the stadium, so do check in advance before visiting.

Museum entry on match days is only for match or event ticket holders. On Mondays, the museum is closed and tours do not run.

As of late 2017, the museum is temporarily closed for construction works.

Dining

London boasts of an ever-evolving food scene that always keeps things fresh and exciting.

In London, top hotels put in their best effort year after year to outdo each other by offering the tastiest afternoon teas, restaurants come up with inventive concepts to attract customers, and new chefs and kitchen talents are constantly emerging from all corners of the city.

If our dining recommendations in the neighbourhood guides were not enough to satisfy your cravings, there are even more in this section.

We cover afternoon tea, luxury dining experiences, and affordable places to eat, giving you even more choices of where to dine.

Afternoon Tea

Afternoon tea, which is a common tradition today, owes its origins to Anna, the 7th Duchess of Bedford.

The tradition isn't as old as many would expect. In the 1800s, at a time when it was normal to eat only early morning breakfast and late evening dinner daily, Anna, irritated by the hunger each day as a result of no lunch, decided to take time out to take tea and snack each afternoon.

Her daily practice was first done alone but over time, friends, relatives, associates and acquaintances followed suit, and the practice has become a tradition among the middle class today.

Afternoon tea is a charming, relaxing, tradition but in reality most Londoners do not have the time for this. However, almost everywhere you look in central London will offer this traditional delight.

Where to go
According to the 2017 Afternoon Tea Awards, the best London Afternoon Tea spot is the Hotel Cafe Royal (68 Regent St, Soho, London W1B 4DY) on Regent Street. A classic, traditional hotel where Oscar Wilde, Winston Churchill and Davie have stayed. The afternoon tea here is very traditional and starts at £55.

Other notable and awarding-winning spots are:

* **Claridge's** *(Brook Street, London, W1K 4HR; 0207 629 8860; www.claridges. co.uk)* in Mayfair is one of the most famous locations for afternoon tea in London, with many people arguing it is the best. Afternoon tea starts at £60 per person.

* **The Ritz** *(150 Piccadilly, London, E1J 9BR; 0207 493 8181; www.theritzlondon. com)* may well be known as the best location in London for afternoon tea, and was where The Queen Mother would come for hers. The quality, service and interiors of the building are simply stunning. Afternoon tea here begins at £57 per person.

* **Landmark Hotel in Marylebone** *(222 Marylebone Road, London, NW1 6JQ; 0207 631 8000; www.landmarklondon. co.uk)*, where the price for afternoon tea starts at £45.

* **Goring Hotel** (Beeston Place, London, SW1W 0JW, 0207 396 9000, www. thegoring.com). Afternoon tea is excellent here. Prices range from £49 to £69, depending on the package requested.

* **Browns Hotel in Mayfair** *(33 Albemarle Street, Mayfair, Greater London, W1S 4BP; 0207 493 6020; www.roccofortehotels.com)* serves afternoon tea with prices starting at £55. A Gluten Free Afternoon Tea is available here.

* **Four Seasons Hotel** just off Park Lane *(Hamilton Place, London W1J 7D; 0207 499 0888; www. fourseasons.com)* offers its afternoon tea from £42.

* **Capital Hotel** in Knightsbridge *(22-24 Basil Street, Knightsbridge, London, SW3 1AT; 0207 589 5171; www.capitalhotel. co.uk)*, serves traditional afternoon tea for £29.50, with a glass of champagne available for an extra £10.

* **Corinthia Hotel** by the Embankment and the river Thames *(Whitehall Place, London SW1A 2BD; 0207 930 8181; www.corinthia. com)* serves afternoon tea, starting at £50 per person.

The Savoy, The Montague on the Gardens, The Langham, The Anthenaeum, The Lanesborough, and **The Connaught** are other notable locations that offer wonderful afternoon tea experiences.

For all the above locations, reservations are either mandatory or highly recommended. For some locations (e.g. The Ritz) you will need to book at least four months in advance, at others last minute tea sittings may be available.

A smart casual dress code applies to all locations. That means no shorts, sportswear, or cut off tank top-style vests; for most places a jacket and tie are optional for men. Jeans are also controversial and may not be permitted at some locations.

Trainers/sneakers are also not allowed in most locations - you will need dressier shoes. At The Ritz a jacket and tie are compulsory for men.

Tea times vary between locations, but you can generally find afternoon tea served between 14:00 and 17:00 daily.

Please note that many locations will now also add an additional 12.5% service charge onto your bill.

Affordable Afternoon Tea

There are some bargain spots that offer afternoon tea for visitors on a budget. Places like the **National Portrait Gallery Restaurant**, offer great afternoon tea at the cost of £27.50, while the **Great Court Restaurant** in the British Museum goes for £19.50 and the **Millbank Lounge** (at the DoubleTree by Hilton London Westminster) goes for £21.95 per person.

Finally, two pubs in central London offer an affordable experience at £10.95 in each – **The Cambridge** *(93 Charing Cross Road, London, WC2H 0DP; 0207 494 0338)*, and **The Wellington in Covent Garden** *(351 Strand, London, WC2R 0HS; 0207 836 2789)*. For the pubs, do call ahead to make sure afternoon tea is being offered on your visit date.

If you don't want the full afternoon tea experience, Cream Tea may be for you and offers a smaller portion size for a small price. Generally, Cream Tea omits the sandwiches included in the full afternoon tea experiences in favour of sweet bites such as scones.

At the **British Museum's Great Court Restaurant**, for example, Cream Tea costs just £8.50.

Luxury Dining

The busy streets of London are filled with bars and eateries, which serve all budgets.

Here we look at the upper end of the scale as we delve into the luxurious world of wining and dining in London.

Whether you are celebrating something special like a birthday, an engagement, an anniversary or just want to spoil yourself, London offers incredible culinary wizardry.

The city is home to many impressive and innovative chefs and it has even been dubbed the culinary "Capital of the World". Below are some of our favourite luxury dining locations in London.

As with afternoon tea, a smart casual dress code applies. Some locations may require that gentlemen wear dinner jackets to enter. Reservations are strongly recommended at most locations; in some places they are mandatory.

It is common practice for many high-end restaurants to add a 12.5% or 15% "discretionary" service charge to your bill. If you feel the service was not up to standard, you may ask for it to be removed as it is optional.

Alain Ducasse at The Dorchester Hotel
(53 Park Lane, London, W1K 1QA; 0207 629 8866; www.alainducasse-dorchester.com)

This three Michelin star restaurant headed by Chef Christophe Moret, offers top notch French cuisine and is a bit like stepping across the channel into France. The three-course a la carte menu starts at £100, four courses are £120, and a seven course tasting menu is £140. The lunch hour menu provides fantastic value, with a three-course meal including two glasses of wine priced at £65.

sketch – Lecture Room and Library
(9 Conduit Street, Mayfair, W1S 2XG; 0207 659 4500; www.sketch.london)

A two Michelin star restaurant located in Mayfair, and partly owned by thirteen Michelin-starred chef, Pierre Gagnaire. Taster menus start from £120 (£95 for the vegetarian tasting menu), while mains start at around £47. This is some of the most expensive food in London. The impressive wine list reaffirms the upscale nature of the restaurant, with wines prices all the way up to £17,000 a bottle.

L'Atelier de Joël Robuchon
(13-15 West Street, London, WC2H 9NE; 0207 010 8600; www.joelrobuchon.co.uk)

This French restaurant, opened in 2006 by the renowned French chef Joël Robuchon, applies several French techniques to an affluent combination of ingredients from differing countries all over the world. This two Michelin star restaurant, offers meals that can easily top £200, as well as some more affordable options.

The 'Menu du Jour' offered at Lunch and pre-theatre is priced reasonably at £45 for three courses, and £65 for five courses. A £29 3-course lunch menu is also available. On the a la Carte menu mains are priced at £29 to £51. The eight-course taster menu is £149.

Restaurant Gordon Ramsay
(68 Royal Hospital Road, London, SW3 4HP; 0207 352 4441; www.gordonramsay restaurants.com/restaurant-gordon-ramsay)

This is one of only a couple of restaurants in London and holds three Michelin stars. The restaurant offers some of the best culinary encounters in the country, and has been named the "Best Restaurant in the UK" on several occasions. A three course lunch menu is available for £65, with an all-day set menu available for £110. A seven-course Prestige Menu is £145.

Affordable Dining

London is a melting point for people from all financial backgrounds. From the ultra-rich to the not so well off. While life in the city may not be getting any cheaper, people's appetite for great value food has never been higher, and with the cost of travel and rent taking ever-growing chunks of people's salaries, finding the city's best budget restaurants is becoming more important than ever before.

Here are some of our favourite, more affordable places to eat that are not fast-food chains.

101 Thai Kitchen
(Stamford Brook Station; 352 King Street, London, W6 0RX; 0208 746 6888; www.101thaikitchen.com)
Located in Haggerston, this joint produces real dishes with origins emanating from northern Thailand. Their green beans, garlic, stir-fried with chilli, beef pad grape and holy basil costs £6.95, while a bowl of tom yum soup goes for £4.95. A meal for two with drinks costs around £35.

Bar Bruno
(Piccadilly Circus Station; 101 Wardour Street, London W1F 0UG; 0207 734 3750)
Located in Soho, one of London's most exclusive addresses, this place has been serving locals and visitors alike for decades. It serves delicious Italian food, as well as British classics, in large portions and may just be our favourite place for a budget meal in central London. £25 will easily get you a meal for two, with cash to spare. Open from 6:00 to 22:00 daily, there is always something delicious to eat here all times of the day.

Wong Kei
(Piccadilly Circus Station; 41-43 Wardour Street, London, W1D 6PY; 0207 437 8408; www.wongkeilondon.com)

Until recently Wong Kei was known for its waiters' terrible attitudes – but this has gotten (slightly) better over recent years. It even became a bit of a tourist attraction in its own right because of its reputation. What is sure is that Wong Kei provides tasty Chinese dishes, huge portions and very low prices. A unique experience. Cash only.

There are a lot of other affordable places to eat in London and some of them include: **Canton Diner** in Chinatown, **The Clutch** in Haggerston, **Regency Café** in Kentish town, and **Tonkotsu East** in Soho. **Vapiano** is one of one our favourite Italian chains and has three locations across central London.

Borough Market and **Camden Market** are the two definitive places to get fresh food from all around the world in minutes. The choice at both markets is huge and they are open for lunch year-round. Whether you fancy British, Portuguese, Indian, French, Jamaican or Chinese, there is something for everyone here. Addresses for both these markets are in the neighbourhood section of this guide.

Saving Money in London

London is without a doubt one of the most expensive cities in the world, but your visit to the city does not have to leave a hole in your pocket. Here are our top tips on how to save money.

❶ Save on Flights and Accommodation

When making flight reservations, check both official airline websites, as well as travel brokers. Websites like expedia.com, skyscanner.net and kayak.com search many sellers at once. Could a stopover, for example, save you hundreds of pounds? Or changing your arrival or departure airport?

Your accommodation has a big effect on how much you spend on your trip, especially for longer stays. Ask: How central do I want to be? What amenities do I need? Am I loyal to a certain brand? Once you have answered those, go to a hotel comparison website such as hotels.com, expedia.com or booking.com. Check them all for the best deal as rooms are often sold through different websites at different prices, and savings can be substantial.

Do you need a luxury hotel or will a budget chain like a TravelLodge, Holiday Inn, or EasyHotel do? With a budget chain, the savings can be huge. Other affordable chains include Novotel, Ibis Budget and Premier Inn - CitizenM is also excellent.

Airbnb.com is another option for travellers, where you can rent out a room in someone's house, or an entire apartment. These can be cheaper than hotel rooms and in the case of apartments you will likely get more for your money. t also allows you to cook your own meals, saving money there too. You can save at least £25 on your Airbnb via our exclusive link - www.airbnb.co.uk/c/gdacosta16.

Lastly, there is couch surfing – a free, or minimal cost opportunity – orchestrated online to, quite literally, crash on someone's couch. While this may be a viable option, note that Londoners are used to less space than many people around the world. If you need a lot of privacy and quiet, this is probably not the best option.

Finally, get travel insurance before leaving home, so if you have a problem you will be covered. This may add to the cost of your trip by a little bit, but will save you a lot of money if something goes wrong.

❷ Arriving in London

Once you have hopped off the plane, you need to make your way to your accommodation, do you need a taxi to get you there? Or will a train or bus be cheaper, and possibly even quicker? Pre-book your train tickets to save money too. For large groups, public transport may work out more expensive than the equivalent journey in a cab.

❸ Vouchers and Coupons

Restaurants, attractions and even shops compete for your custom. Look out for vouchers and coupons which can save you a bit of money. You may find these online, in leaflets at hotels and tourist information centres. Whether it is a percentage off, or a set amount of money, it all adds up over your trip to London.

❹ Attractions and Museums

Most cultural attractions and museums are free admission in London, which is fantastic. For attractions which charge admission fees, visit the attraction's website and pre-purchase your tickets. This usually saves you money over the 'on the day' gate price.

Be sure to check whether attractions have partnered with each other too, or whether they are part of the same company. Partnered attractions usually offer ticket combo deals where you purchase tickets for several attractions at once at a discount price. A good example are the attractions operated by Merlin Entertainments such as the London Eye, London Dungeon, London Aquarium, Madame Tussauds, and Shrek's Adventure – you can get combination tickets for all of these and save up to 40%.

❺ Save BIG money on attractions by 'travelling by train'

Here is a big secret: National Rail offers a "Days Out" promotion with 2 for 1 deals on a huge number of major London attractions. This involves you travelling by rail to London in order to get the discount.

If you are already in London, however, you can still take advantage of this offer. First of all, visitdaysoutguide.co.uk and browse the offers available and print vouchers for attractions you wish to visit. Then, visit any London National Rail Station (note: not Underground stations, but National Rail) such as Waterloo, King's Cross, St. Pancras, London Bridge, etc. Go to a ticket machine and purchase a cheap ticket from anywhere else to London as the destination – get the cheapest ticket possible. Usually there will be one for a few pounds.

Then, present your train ticket and printed voucher at your chosen attraction's entrance for 2 for 1 entry. This works at major attractions such as The Tower of London, London Eye, Madame Tussauds, Thames Clippers and Hampton Court Palace.

❻ Consider a London Pass

If you plan to visiting a lot of London attractions, consider getting a London Pass – this is a one-fee pass that includes entry into many of London's major attractions and tours, with over sixty to choose. It even includes a one-day hop-on, hop-off bus ticket.

Note that the London Eye, London Dungeon, London Aquarium, Shrek's Adventure and Madame Tussauds are not included in the London Pass, and neither is The Shard. Some attractions will grant you express entry with the London Pass. Adult prices are £62 for one day, £85 for 2 days, £101 for 3 days, £139 for 6 days and £169 for 10 days. Child prices are at least £20 cheaper. We advise against getting the Travelcard add-on as this works out more expensive than getting an Oyster Card yourself.

❼ Getting around London

If using public transport within London, get an Oyster Card or use a contactless payment card for the best value. If you are only staying in central London, consider travelling by bus only instead of the tube - the fare is £1.50 on the bus versus £2.40 on the tube.

If you want a bit of extra privacy, ride-sharing service Uber is a cheaper alternative to the black London cabs.

❽ London Tours

Hop On, Hop Off bus tours are a great way to understand the layout of the city and learn about its history. However, we do not use recommend using them to get between attractions as they often use indirect routes. Once you have understood where everything is, and have enjoyed the commentary, swap to public transport to make the most of your time in London.

Big Bus Tours, Original Sightseeing Tours, Golden Tours and London City Tour are the four big operators. The first three listed are the biggest. Haggle with ticket agents to get the best price, and purchase the shortest ticket length (generally 24 hours). Although the second day may "only be £5 more", the tube and London Buses can get you around for a similar price and more quickly.

Many of these companies sell their tickets as 24, 48 and 72-hour tickets. However, be aware that the last tours usually depart between 16:30 and 19:00 depending on the season. The 12-hours they are shut for service are rarely mentioned. Ticket agents can also get you discounted attraction tickets once you have a bus tour ticket.

Alternatively, there are countless walking tour companies offering a variety of tours. If you are unsure, consider one of the free walking tour companies out there – FreeToursByFoot.com and FreeLondonWalkingTours.com allow you to choose your own price per tour after you have taken them. We recommend £10 per person as a good benchmark for a two-hour tour.

9 Save money when shopping

London is renowned for its luxury shopping, but there are also fantastic bargains to be had. You should always shop around as competition is fierce - what may be £40 in one shop, may just be £25 further down the road.

The Boxing Day sales start on 26th December each year. On Boxing Day, shoppers usually begin queuing up outside big London stores before the sun rises to get the best bargains when the shops open. At other times, keep an eye out for sales signs.

10 Save on Theatre Tickets

A trip to London would not be complete without taking in a West End show. However, these can be very expensive, and the priciest seats sell for upwards of £65 each. Theatres have more affordable ticket options available, with the cheapest seats starting at £15.

Most theatres also offer 'day seats' (often the front row), sold daily at the theatres' box office for shows the same day. These are usually well priced (£30 maximum). See an app called TodayTix for a digital version of this.

TKTS, located in Leicester Square, is another fantastic option. Open year-round, this theatre ticket booth is the official seller of tickets for all of London's shows. Plus, you can save up to 50% on shows if you buy the tickets on the day of performance. Check their website at www.tkts.co.uk to see which tickets are on sale for the same day and up to 2 further days in advance.

Finally, twice a year, the theatres join together for discount events. In January and February, getintolondontheatre.co.uk offers amazing deals for £10-£40 on big shows, whereas kidsweek.co.uk offers 'kids go free' deals to shows in August (up to the age of 16). Tickets must be pre-booked online and carry no booking fees.

2018 Seasonal Events

*London always has something interesting and different going on whenever you visit.
Here is a month by month list of some the events throughout the year.*

January
New Year's Day Parade - 1st January 2018
Over 10,000 performers take to the streets of London on New Year's Day to celebrate in style. Having been performed yearly since 1987, this event gets over 600,000 spectators each year and a TV audience of over 300 million worldwide.

The parade route usually starts in Berkley Street (by Green Park), makes its way up to Piccadilly Circus, turns down Haymarket, around Trafalgar Square, down Whitehall, and ends in Parliament Square by Big Ben and the Houses of Parliament. Admission is free. Local roads are usually closed to traffic from 04:00 to 18:00.

February
Chinese New Year - 18th February 2018.
Although Chinese New Year itself is on the 16th February in 2018, the celebrations will be held on the subsequent weekend.

You can celebrate the start of the Year of the Dog all around the West End with events held on Trafalgar Square and Chinatown from 10:00 to 18:00. London's Chinese New Year celebrations are the largest outside Asia, with parades, performances and fireworks. Details may change this year but usually, at 10:00 a large lion parade makes its way from Trafalgar Square to Chinatown; from 12:00 onwards stage performances are held; and at 17:20 there is the grand finale as dancers and acrobats take to the stage, and pyrotechnics illuminate Nelson's Column.

March
St. Patrick's Day Celebrations - 18th March 2018.
Although, St. Patrick's Day is on the 17th March each year, it is traditional for the large celebrations in London to be held on a Sunday. The day celebrates one of the patron Saints of Ireland, and is a national holiday there.

In 2018, Sunday 18th March is the big St Patrick's Day Parade in London, with floats, marching bands from across the UK, sports clubs and Irish dancing schools. The London St Patrick's Day Parade follows the same route as the aforementioned New Year's Day Parade. On Trafalgar Square, there will be Irish food on sale, as well as music and traditional dancing. There are also usually children's activities.

Boat Races - 24th March 2018.
Two different boat races take place along a 4.25-mile (6.8km) stretch of the river Thames.

The "Head of the River Race" runs from Mortlake to Putney.

Over 400 crews of eights take part, making it one of the highest participation events in London. The race was first held in 1926.

The Oxford and Cambridge Races are perhaps more well-known, and race the same route but in the opposite direction – from Putney to Mortlake. The first race took place in 1829 in Henley on Thames, following a challenge between old school friends.

The best place to watch the event is from one of the many pubs that line this section of the river. Admission is free.

April

St. George's Day Celebrations - 2018 dates to be confirmed
St. George, the patron Saint of England, is celebrated every year in Trafalgar Square. The event is free to attend and usually involves food stalls serving traditional English fare, free activities and shows, and activities for kids too.

St. George's Day is celebrated on April 23rd, but dates for the annual celebration on Trafalgar Square have not yet been revealed.

London Marathon - 22nd April 2018
Whether you fancy running yourself, or watching and supporting others, the London Marathon will get you into the running spirit. The marathon takes place all over central, east and south London with major road closures all across the city from approximately 07:00 to 19:00. Charges apply to enter the Marathon. Running places are balloted and they usually sell out over 6 months in advance. Spectators do not need a ticket.

May

Museums at Night - 16th to 19th May 2018
Museums at Night is where several museums, galleries and heritage sites throughout the UK throw open their doors after hours to showcase their treasures in unexpected ways. Museums that have participated in the event in the past include: London Museum of Water and Steam, Horniman Museum and Gardens, and Banqueting House. More information is available at museumsatnight.org.uk.

The RHS Chelsea Flower Show - 22nd to 26th May 2018
The Chelsea Flower Show has been held in the grounds of the Royal Hospital Chelsea, London every year since 1913. It is an extremely popular event where designers, local councils and individuals compete to design the most beautiful and interesting garden.

With over 150,000 visitors each year, tickets must be purchased in advance due to the limited capacity at the event grounds. Innovative winning gardens in recent years include James May's garden made entirely of plasticine, and Diarmuid Gavin's Irish Sky Garden, the first garden to be suspended in the air. Tickets start at £34 and go up to £74 depending on the date and time of visit.

June
West End Live - 2018 dates unknown
This free annual event showcases the best of the West End in Trafalgar Square. All day Saturday and Sunday you can turn up and see what's on. On stage, the casts of some of London's most well-known shows will be part of live performances.

Eateries, small shops and kids' activities round out this family friendly event. This is a great way to sample a selection of West End shows, and then purchase tickets to the one(s) you enjoy most. In 2017, the event took place on 24th and 25th June.

Pride in London Festival - 7th July 2018
The Pride in London festival, a celebration of the lesbian, gay, bisexual and transgender (LGBT+) community across London as an event continues to increase in size year after year. Performances, speeches and other forms of art will take place throughout the week at various locations around London.

The culmination of the festival, however, is the large scale Pride in London Parade. It travels all the way from Baker Street down to Trafalgar Square.

July
Prudential Ride London - 27th to 29th July 2018
Prudential Ride London is a world-class festival of cycling. FreeCycle is a 10-mile track around central London's famous landmarks with roads closed to cars. You can join the route at any point, do as many laps as you like and come and go as you please. Cyclists can stop off en route to enjoy bike-based entertainment and activities all around central London. You can either sign up in advance or turn up on the day.

There are also four different competitive races that take place over the course of the weekend; some races span up to 200km in length! A Cycling Show will also take place in East London at the Excel Centre.

BBC Proms - 13th July to 8th September 2018
This classic musical festival, hosted by the BBC at the Royal Albert Hall, is a delight to attend. With standing tickets only costing £7.50 each, the aim is to bring live classical music within the reach of all. Tickets for seats start at £16.

On the last night of the show, as so many people want to see the finale, the solution has been to set up giant screens – dubbed *Proms in the Park* – which allow you to watch the same spectacle, but outdoors in Hyde Park.

August
Notting Hill Carnival - 25th to 27th August 2018
Each year in August, Notting Hill is home to the world's second-biggest carnival – Notting Hill Carnival – where London's West Indian communities gather to put on a street festival that is a joy to experience, and is filled with fantastic photo opportunities. From the colourful costumes and floats on the main parade, to the Caribbean food and live music, this event is a huge amount of fun, with people from all backgrounds celebrating together.

September
Open House Weekend London - 22nd and 23rd September 2018
Open House Weekend was created to open up London's incredible buildings to the general public who don't otherwise have access. Today, it has hundreds of locations participating. It is as much about looking at historic buildings, as it is about a look towards the future.

Buildings and areas open to the public in the past have included Burlington House, the Foreign and Commonwealth Office, Fitzrovia Chapel, the Royal College of Physicians, and many more.

London Design Festival - 15th to 23rd September 2018
This annual art and design festival is an opportunity to see works from both established and up-and-coming artists. The festival is not confined to one area of London, and has events throughout the city. Exact details on the exhibitions and installations on show were not available at the time of writing, but be sure to check londondesignfestival.com for information closer to the start date.

October
Frieze London - 4th to 7th October 2018
October is another great month for art lovers, as the world-renowned Frieze London event is held. This ticketed event allows you to see contemporary art in Regent's Park.

The festival includes works from 160 galleries from over 25 countries. More information on 2018 exhibitors will be available closer to the festival start date at friezelondon.com.

Diwali: Festival of Lights - 2018 date not yet available
Diwali, also known as the Festival of Lights, is an event which celebrates the triumph of light over dark, and good over evil. The festival is very popular in many Asian countries but is now celebrated by people of all faiths and nationalities in London.

Diwali on Trafalgar Square includes a children's parade, live performances throughout the day, eateries and more. The 2018 date for the event has not yet been revealed. More information will be available closer to the time at diwaliinlondon.com.

November
Christmas Lights Switch On - Early November
London gets into the Christmas spirit quite early in the year, as the Christmas Lights along Oxford Street and Regent Street are turned on a full 6 to 8 weeks before Christmas Day. Both the events are popular and free to attend, and take place on different days. You can expect live music and entertainment, and usually a celebrity appearance. After the switch on, the lights stay on continuously until early January. Exact details are announced in October.

Bonfire Night - 5th November
Bonfire Night is a celebration of the failed plot to blow up Parliament in 1605. Guy Fawkes placed explosives under the House of Lords in order to assassinate King James I. The plot was foiled, and is remembered through an annual celebration. The event usually involves burning an effigy of Guy Fawkes, as well as a large fireworks display. Firework displays can usually be found in Blackheath, Wimbledon Park, Southwark Park, Cleveland Square in Westminster, and others further out of central London. Many of these ask for a small entrance fee or a donation.

Winter Wonderland - 18th November 2017 to 1st December 2018
Located on the Park Lane side of Hyde Park, Winter Wonderland is one of the go-to places during the Christmas season each year. It is a huge well-themed, funfair style attraction. Admission into Winter Wonderland is free, with activities and food charged individually.

Rides are one of the staples of the funfair with everything from ghost trains to helter-skelters. There are also shops with Christmas-themed merchandise, beer tents and places to eat. It is good family fun and worth visiting, but it is often very crowded. Opening times are 10:00 to 22:00 daily. Closed on Christmas Day.

December
Great Christmas Pudding Race - 2nd December 2017
Taking place in Covent Garden, this 35-year-old tradition is a charity event, which sees people trying to complete an obstacle course in the quickest time possible. The catch is that each contestant must carry a Christmas pudding round the course and get it back in perfect condition. This is all done while going up and down slides, through slaloms, and more. This is great fun to watch and a good recommendation for a unique day out.

New Year's Eve - 31st December
London celebrates the arrival of the New Year in style with firework displays all across town. The big one, however, is the Mayor of London's fireworks on the River Thames and the London Eye. Year after year, these fireworks have amazed Londoners and visitors alike, and they are even timed to music. This is an extremely popular event; tickets for viewing areas are required and are available at £10 each - they sell out in advance.

There are views of the fireworks from non-ticketed areas and from further afield but these are less than ideal. Even with a ticket, you will need to get there a few hours early for the best spots.

Maps

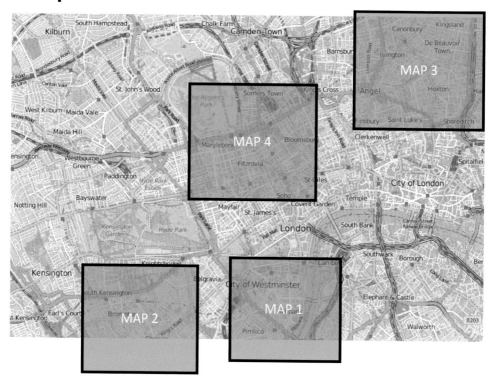

The following pages include maps of London. The map above gives you a general idea of the areas of London which house the most attractions.

These maps are not designed to be used for walking directions, but instead to give you a general sense of where the attractions are located in relation to each other - nevertheless major roads and landmarks are included.

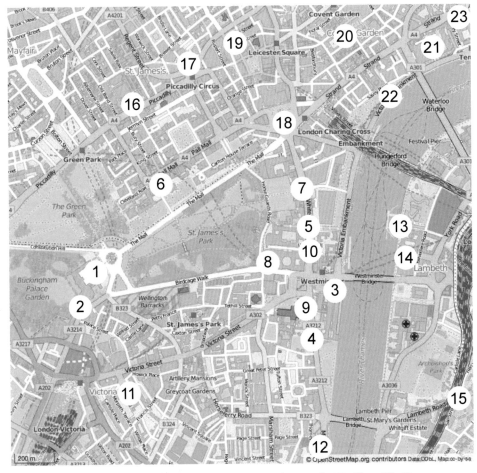

1 - Buckingham Palace

2 - The Queen's Gallery and The Royal Mews

3 - Big Ben & The Houses of Parliament

4 - The Jewel Tower

5 - Downing Street

6 - St. James's Palace

7 - Horse Guards Parade

8 - Churchill War Rooms

9 - Westminster Abbey

10 - The Cenotaph and Banqueting House

11 - Westminster Cathedral

12 - Tate Britain (0.2 miles south of position on map)

13 - London Eye

14 - London Aquarium, London Dungeon and Shrek's Adventure

15 - Imperial War Museum (0.2 miles north-east of position on map)

16 - Royal Academy of Arts

17 - Piccadilly Circus

18 - Trafalgar Square, National Gallery and National Portrait Gallery

19 - Chinatown

20 - Covent Garden and London Transport Museum

21 - Somerset House and Courtauld Gallery

22 - Cleopatra's Needle

23 - Royal Courts of Justice (0.2 miles north-east of position on map)

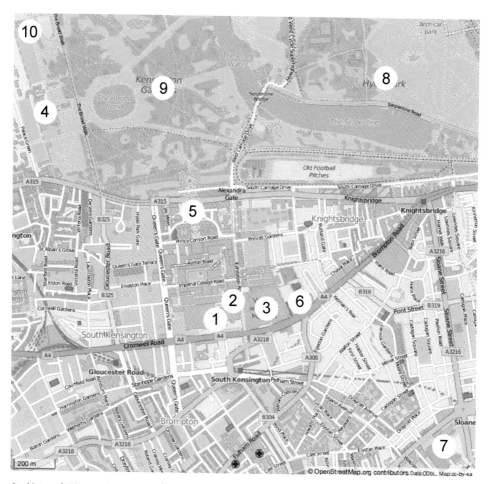

1 - Natural History Museum

2 - Science Museum

3 - Victoria and Albert Museum

4 - Kensington Palace

5 - Royal Albert Hall

6 - Brompton Oratory

7 - Saatchi Gallery

8 - Hyde Park

9 - Kensington Gardens

10 - Portobello Road and Notting Hill (1 mile north-west of position on map)

Map 3: The City and London Bridge

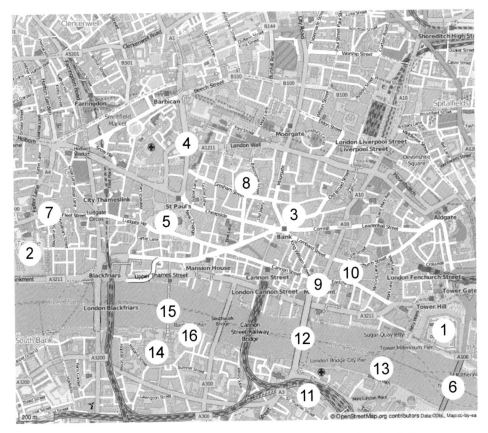

1 - Tower of London	7 - Fleet Street	12 - London Bridge
2 - Inner and Middle Temple	8 - Guildhall Art Gallery	13 - HMS Belfast
3 - Bank of England Museum	9 - The Monument to the Great Fire of London	14 - Tate Modern
4 - Museum of London		15 - The Millennium Bridge
5 - St. Paul's Cathedral	10 - Sky Garden	16 - Shakespeare's Globe Theatre
6 - Tower Bridge	11 - The Shard and The View from The Shard	

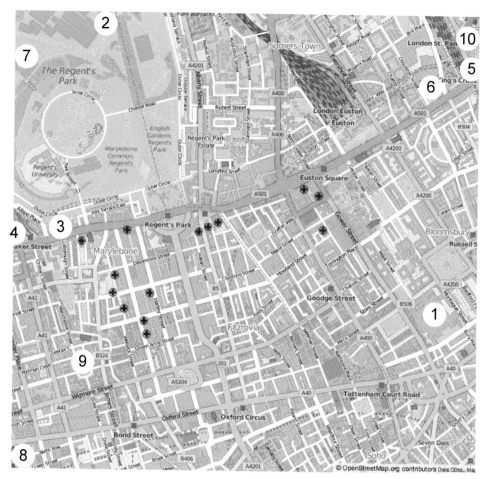

1 - The British Museum

2 - Regent's Park and ZSL London Zoo

3 - Madame Tussauds

4 - The Sherlock Holmes Museum

5 - Harry Potter's Platform 9¾ & Shop

6 - The British Library

7 - Abbey Road Studios (1 mile west of position on map)

8 - Marble Arch

9 - The Wallace Collection

10 - London Canal Museum (0.3 miles north-east of position on map)

95192057R00080

Made in the USA
Middletown, DE
24 October 2018